YOUR CHILD & DRUGS

YOUR CHILD & DRUGS

ROSS CAMPBELL, M.D.
WITH PAT LIKES

VICTOR BOOKS®

A DIVISION OF SCRIPTURE PRESS PUBLICATIONS INC.
USA CANADA ENGLAND

The stories told in this book are based on real case histories. The problems, the pain, and the frustrations are real, however, names and details have been changed to protect the privacy of those whose stories are recounted here.

Recommended Dewey Decimal Classification: 157.6

Suggested Subject Heading: DRUG ABUSE

Library of Congress Catalog Card Number: 88-60221

ISBN: 0-89693-563-9

|CONTENTS|

| PREFACE |

This book is written from my years of experience as a family counselor. It is for parents and anyone else who is involved with kids in any way. It is not just a book for parents of kids using drugs. If your child is fortunate enough to have escaped drug involvement, this book is still for you. If your child is only three years old, and you want a drug-free life for her, this book is also for you. If you are eagerly awaiting the arrival of your first child, this book is certainly for you.

In order for you to understand what you can do, either to correct an existing drug problem or to keep one from developing, you should—I'll even say, you *must*—know what is contained in these chapters. Reading, understanding, and applying this book can help you and your child, indeed your entire family, live drug-free and experience real "highs" in your relationships.

I have tried to set down in a clear way the causes of drug use and abuse. Many parents tend to place the total blame for a child's drug use on themselves, the child's peer group, or society at large. Parents, peers, and society do play major roles in a child's decision to use or abstain from drugs, but no *single* influence can be blamed for a child's decision to use drugs.

Few people understand *all* the underlying reasons for drug

involvement, such as depression, anxiety, anger, and mental/neurological illnesses. This lack of understanding is the main reason why so many parents and other concerned people fail to help kids overcome their drug problems. Far too often I see a young person whose physical addiction is treated while the underlying causes of his drug problem are ignored. The child only *appears* to have been helped. He is soon back on drugs to the dismay and despair of his parents.

In this book I discuss the effective "dual diagnosis" approach which looks at *all* the reasons for drug abuse. This approach also sees the child's drug habit as a family problem. The evaluation and treatment process, which should involve a number of professionals, is designed to build family ties and to help the child find a happy, meaningful life without drugs.

Throughout this book I have sought to give you a detailed guide to the proper kind of treatment for a child with a drug problem. I have explained a number of reasons why kids, even kids from the "best" families, become involved in drugs. I have also explained how you can prevent that involvement.

Drug abuse has become an extremely serious problem in Western society. It becomes a personal tragedy when your child gets involved with drugs. I have written this book to help you and your child end or avoid the tragedy of drug abuse.

Ross Campbell, M.D.
January 15, 1988

|ESSENTIAL DEFINITIONS|

Before you begin to read this book, I'd like you to be familiar with a few terms.

Addiction—physiological dependence on a drug. Addiction reflects bodily changes that stem from prolonged use of certain drugs.

Anger—a feeling of displeasure resulting from injury, mistreatment, opposition, etc., and usually showing itself in a desire to fight back at the supposed cause of this feeling.

Anxiety—an inner state of tension characterized by rapid heartbeat, shortness of breath, and other manifestations of autonomic nervous system arousal; a general emotional response to stress; a negative emotion characterized by persistent fear and dread.

Authoritarian—characterized by demanding unquestioning obedience to authority, rather than allowing individual freedom of judgment and action.

Authoritative—having or showing authority; official.

Biochemical—chemical makeup and transactions of the brain.

Bipolar affective disorder—severe mental disorder characterized by radical mood swings between elation and depression, also called manic depressive psychosis. Occasionally this disorder may be seen with elation or depression alone.

Borderline personality disorder—characterized by instability and drastic mood shifts; such individuals are impulsive and at

9

times may appear psychotic.

Dependence—a psychological and social reason for problem usage of drugs.

Depression—emotional state of dejection, feelings of gloom and of worthlessness.

Drug—a habit-forming substance that directly affects the brain and nervous system and changes mood, perception, and/or consciousness.

Drug abuse—misuse or overuse of a drug to the point that it becomes a panacea or the central focus of the individual's life.

Dyslexia—partial inability to read or to understand what one reads silently or aloud.

Manic depressive psychosis—(see Bipolar affective disorder)

Metabolic—of, involving, characterized by, or resulting from metabolism.

Metabolism—chemical and physical processes continuously going on in living organisms and cells by which assimilated food is built into protoplasm and then used and broken down into simpler substances or waste matter, releasing energy for all vital processes.

Neurohormonal—central nervous system hormones primarily located in the brain. These brain hormones are neurotransmitters and are responsible for transmitting electrical impulses from one nerve ending to another.

Neurology—the study of brain and nervous system and disorders thereof.

Neurological handicaps—organic brain dysfunctions caused by actual tissue damage or dysfunction of the brain.

Passive-aggressive behavior—suppressed anger that comes out unconsciously from a child or adult in a negative way.

Perceptual handicap—a handicap which causes an individual to perceive visual and audio messages in a way that can be detrimental to his understanding of the messages. (Dyslexia is a perceptual handicap.)

Psychomotor—involving both psychological and physical activity.

Somatic—of the body as distinguished from the soul or mind.

Toxicity—the poisonous nature of a substance.

Our Drug Culture

Let's start this chapter by seeing how much you know about the drug scene. Answer each question "true" or "false," then check your answers as you read the chapter.

True   False

1. Experimentation is harmless and often promotes disinterest in drugs.
2. Kids of the sixties used drugs more than kids use them today.
3. Most kids don't become interested in drugs until they are fifteen or sixteen years old.
4. Nicotine is one of the most addictive chemicals known to man.
5. Kids turn to their peers more often

than their parents when they need
help and guidance.
6. Seeking help too early for your
child's drug problem can worsen the
situation.

Now let me introduce you to three people you will read a lot about in this book.

Johnny Alton is a tall, handsome, fifteen-year-old boy. He constantly jerks his head, flipping his long, black hair out of his eyes. He does not like school except for photography class. He likes to play the guitar.

"Dr. Campbell, did you know that my old man hides his booze under the blankets on the closet shelf upstairs? I see him go up there all the time and take a swig, but he don't know it. And when Mom finds his bottles, she always blames me.

"And then my old man says, 'Hey, Johnny, you been drinkin' again?' Then Mom gets in on it and they both start yellin' at me.

"My mom accuses me 'cause she don't like thinkin' my dad drinks. Listen, man, I don't drink! I can find stuff better than that to get high on."

Concerned people at Johnny's school have urged his parents to get him into a treatment program. His mother is agreeable, but his father doesn't want to get involved. A lot of truth would have to come out if he did.

■

Sixteen-year-old Larry Schmidt is talking to his friend in the lunchroom of a local school. "I got promoted to the bakery at that store where I work."

"Neat," his friend replied. "Now you'll really be makin' the bread."

"Ha, ha," Larry sneered. "Funny, funny. Listen, man, now I can save my money to buy better weed." As Larry leaned to the floor to retrieve a pencil, two white pills rolled from his shirt pocket.

Four or five kids gathered around his table. "Hey, Dude, you've got white cross. Give us some."

"No way, man. I party all night and I gotta have something to keep me awake all day. But maybe I can get you some. Meet me at Al's after school."

■

Evelyn Williams is a recently divorced, working mother of two teenage daughters. She attends church irregularly, taking one, sometimes both of the girls. Two years ago her medical doctor prescribed a low dosage of Valium for her to help her get through the emotional trauma of a major surgery and the loss of her job.

Soon after Evelyn started taking the Valium, Peggy, her pony-tailed fourteen-year-old, came home from school in tears.

"Oh, Mother, I didn't make cheerleader," she lamented. "I think I'll just die!"

"Now, Peggy, let's calm down. I have supper ready. It's your favorite."

"Is food all you can think of at a time like this?" Peggy yelled. "How can I possibly eat?" With that, she ran crying to her room and slammed the door.

Peggy's hurt was painful to Evelyn. She didn't like seeing her daughter so upset, and she really wasn't up to any hassles herself. Knowing the calming effect of her Valium, she gave a tablet to Peggy. "There now Peg, you'll soon feel much better."

Soon, each time Peggy had a problem, the simplest solution was a pill. This introduction to Valium led Peggy into an increased usage of the drug, experimentation with other drugs, and finally, drug addiction. Evelyn did not realize that her seemingly innocent action would lead to her daughter's drug addiction.

■

I'll come back to Johnny, Larry, Evelyn, and Peggy after a

few pages. Right now let's look at some hard facts about the drug scene.

Experimental Drug Use

Experimental beginnings can and do lead to life-threatening addiction. By age eighteen, approximately 60 percent of today's kids will have experimented with drugs, a 6,000 percent increase over the last twenty years. In the sixties, less than 1 percent of American teens had ever tried marijuana or any other kind of illicit drug. Now, smoking pot has become a sort of rite of passage into teenage social life. Think about this: the average age of first use has dropped from nineteen years of age in the sixties to twelve years of age for the kids of the eighties. Today "Let's go party" means let's get high on drugs and alcohol. Forty percent of America's teens have become "social" or regular users. Most of these are addicted or totally dependent on drugs. Ten percent of America's high school seniors come to school stoned every day. Fifty percent of all high school dropouts and truants are regular drug users (*Drug Scene Update*, PRIDE, [National Parents' Resource Institute for Drug Education, Inc.] 1987).

These young people carry their habits into the work force and the military. Ten percent of our nation's work force abuses drugs and alcohol (*Today Show*, July 24, 1987). Studies show a decline in economic productivity and national security directly due to abuse of illicit drugs.

Ten years ago, I could say that limited experimentation with drugs would not be damaging. I could say that those kids who were experimenting would mature, grow out of the desire to use drugs, and go on to have productive, healthy lives. Not so today. With the introduction of "crack," experimentation can be fatal or lead to complete addiction within six weeks. Sadly, kids can become addicted (if not to crack within six weeks) to any other drug within the period of one summer vacation. And since growing adolescents can become addicted to a drug much faster than an adult, experimentation is no longer something that can be ignored.

Teachers are worried. They are seeing mentally and physically healthy young people leave their classrooms in the spring only to return in the fall as glassy eyed, totally drug dependent individuals.

These kids do not realize that *every illicit external chemical known to produce changes in the nervous system also damages that system. There are no exceptions. There are no consequence-free drugs.*

The Path to Drug Abuse

Kids who abuse drugs usually follow a pattern. Eighty-five percent of those who experiment with cigarettes will become addicted to nicotine even after smoking sometimes as few as five to ten cigarettes. Of these kids, 81 percent will try marijuana whereas only 21 percent of nonsmokers will try marijuana.

Smoking marijuana becomes the springboard for heavier drug use. Sixty-seven percent of marijuana users progress to other drugs, while 98 percent of those teens who do not smoke pot also do not take other drugs. Young girls who take stimulants in the form of diet pills also go on to use illicit drugs.

A teen who drinks alcohol is two or three times more likely to become an alcoholic than an adult who drinks. This vulnerability is explained by immature metabolic and neurological systems. Until the age of physical maturity is reached, usually nineteen for boys and twenty-three for girls, the body does not metabolize alcohol effectively. Adolescents are also vulnerable to alcohol dependence because their brain systems are not completely organized, and their bodies are not fully developed (*Drug Scene Update*, PRIDE, 1987).

Alcohol is a deadly drug. It has deleterious effects and attacks the nervous system. Not only is it a dangerous drug, but it is also legal and accepted by the general population. Daily use of alcohol is not termed unusual in today's society.

Alcohol is a subtle drug. Most alcoholics do not realize that they have a problem, nor do their friends. Drinking is accepted by our children because they see most adults drink. Alcohol is displayed in almost all stores, on TV, and in movies. Yet, it is not any safer than any other drug. Over a period of time, it can shorten a person's life. Alcohol destroys the body.

Experimental Drug Use Can't Be Ignored

Children who experiment with cigarettes expose themselves to nicotine, one of the most addictive chemicals. They are likely to develop a dependency on cigarettes, a difficult habit to break. The younger the age of the beginning smoker, the greater the chances of serious health impairment. For example, in addition to encouraging use of illicit drugs, cigarette smoking also leads to cancers of the lungs, throat, and bladder (*Drug Scene Update*, PRIDE, 1987).

Those who experiment with marijuana will also harm their bodies. According to PRIDE, "The increasing potency in commercially cultivated marijuana is associated with more rapid and serious deterioration of mental and physical health. . . . Marijuana intoxication has lingering effects on psychomotor function, long after the 'high' has worn off. The complex actions of the 421 known chemicals in the plant . . . are responsible for the system-wide biological impairment observed in marijuana abusers" (*Drug Scene Update*, PRIDE, 1987).

Considering how dangerous these drugs of initial experimentation are, you can readily see that any sign of drug use in your child cannot be ignored. I realize that adolescents are difficult to talk with at times so I am not suggesting that you immediately jump at them with "Hey, I know you're on drugs. You need help!" These kids feel insecure enough about themselves without well-meaning parents accusing them of using drugs.

Early teen years are difficult for the teen. It is the most accelerated period of human growth, except for the first eighteen months of life. Cells and body tissue are either altered or replaced altogether during these adolescent years. Sexual potency, nearly all of one's skeletal stature, and the capacity for abstract thinking develop during this time of life.

Adolescence is also a stage of awkwardness. A croaking voice, a beard, breasts, body hair—all of these either arriving too early or too late—can be sources of devastating self-doubt.

The best rule to follow, if you are concerned that your child might be experimenting with drugs, is to gradually develop a conversation about drugs. Ask your adolescent how he feels about using drugs, or if he has ever been put in the uncomfortable situation of having been offered drugs. If he becomes extremely defensive, then you might have cause to check into the situation more closely. Try to become acquainted with all his friends and keep abreast of all his activities.

Adolescents want their parents to be involved in their lives, but they are the last ones to make that desire obvious. The life of an adolescent can be, and often is, "the pits." Someone once said that the only way out of adolescence is through it. I heartily agree.

Living through adolescence, as difficult as it may seem, can produce some wonderful adults. But pity the adolescent—and this could be your child—who chooses to get through this period by anesthetizing himself with chemicals. He only delays the process of maturity or inhibits it altogether.

Don't wait until your child is a teenager to start a discussion of drugs. Proverbs 22:6 (NIV) commands us to "train a child in the way he should go, and when he is old he will not turn from it."

It is easy and extremely important to discuss drugs with your young child, but don't overemphasize the subject. Just wait until the subject comes up on TV, in the movies, or when a famous sports figure is highlighted on the news because of a drug problem. These are all perfect times to begin a calm discussion of drugs. Let your child know how important he is and that drugs are certainly not in your dreams for his future. Be careful not to become loud and accusatory. Don't threaten your child or teen with useless statements, such as, "I'll never talk to you again if I ever catch you using drugs!" This type of threat only invites trouble because it cannot be carried out. It only creates anger. Empty threats are useless child-rearing techniques.

No Child Is Immune
Whether we like to admit it or not, we are a "drug culture." If you have an adolescent in your home, she will in some way come in contact with drugs. Even though peers do not actually force your child to use drugs, peer association may be the

source of initial drug acquaintance. The man in the pin-striped suit with the big car parked in the alley, or the "tough gang" from the other side of town may also expose your child to drugs. But more likely your child will learn about drugs from careless parents or dear Uncle Henry who, just for the fun of it, mixes your thirteen-year-old her first drink. A nationwide study of adults informs us that two thirds of those adults surveyed use alcohol and nicotine at least twice a week (*Young Adolescents and Their Parents*, Search Institute Project Report, 1984, p. 262). So, you see, drugs are all around your child. Drug addiction, drug dependency, and the use of recreational drugs are a fact of life for millions of today's kids. No child is immune.

Recently, a friend told me about finding an adolescent girl lying across his driveway when he arrived home from work one evening. "I didn't know what to think, Ross," he said. "At first I just thought she was trying to play a joke on one of my girls, so I went on into the house.

"I called to Joni, my daughter, and told her that Jeri was out on the driveway. Before I could say any more, Joni cried, 'Oh, no, Daddy. I just talked to her a minute ago on the phone and told her to go to bed, and I would be right over. She's drunk. She called me and told me that she drank an awful lot of some kind of liquor she found in her dad's liquor cabinet.'

"I hurried outside with Joni, and we helped Jeri into the house. Then I called her mother and made her aware of the situation. I was concerned for the girl's health. She's only fourteen, and she must have consumed a lot of alcohol because we could hardly get her to walk or talk.

"I can't imagine what made her do a thing like that. That kid has everything. Both her parents work and give her anything she wants."

My friend was surprised that something like that could happen to a friend of his daughter. He was under the impression that drug or alcohol use and abuse affected other people but would never touch his family. He was upset about his daughter associating with someone who would get drunk, or who even had access to alcohol.

The Peer Pressure Excuse

Kim, a blue-eyed, high school freshman, sat tensely across from me in my office. "How are things going, Kim?" I asked in an attempt to get a conversation started.

"OK, I guess," she replied quietly. "Only Mom and me—well, we argue a lot about my best friend, Sarah."

Kim had been coming to our clinic on a weekly basis for three weeks now, and I learned early in our sessions that she found it difficult to express her feelings. She fell silent again. "I'm a good listener if you'd like to tell me about it, Kim," I told her. "Maybe between the two of us, we can figure something out that will help you and your mother."

"Well, she thinks that Sarah forced me to drink, and she won't let Sarah come over anymore." Kim looked pleadingly at me. "Dr. Campbell, Sarah doesn't drink—she doesn't do any kind of drugs, honest. But I can't make my mom believe that. How can I make her believe that?"

Kim's story is all too typical. A popular myth today is that peer pressure is the reason any kid uses drugs, including alcohol; however, if you ask kids who have an insight into drug problems, they will deny that the reason for the problem is peer pressure. Kim knew that her friend, Sarah, didn't *make* her drink alcohol. Sure, both girls knew that it was available within their peer group, but it was not being *forced* on anyone. Kim had discovered, by experimenting herself, that alcohol could make her feel good. It could block the feelings of sadness and loneliness that she was experiencing.

You see, Kim has an underlying problem, which is depression. Neither she nor her parents recognized her real problem. Her parents found it convenient to blame Kim's friends for her involvement with alcohol. In this case, peers entered the picture after the fact. Kim was feeling low, so a few of her friends suggested that a couple of drinks of alcohol could make her feel better. Nobody forced her; they were just there (and peers are "there" much more than parents) when the curiosity and/or the need arose. And Kim's "need" came about due to her long-standing inability to communicate with her parents. She felt lonely and isolated, so she was a prime candidate for experimentation.

Fortunately for Kim, her parents became aware of her problem. The entire family has been counseling with us, and we are making progress in clearing up many misunderstandings. Kim's family is getting reacquainted, and her experimentation with alcohol should soon be behind her.

Like Kim, most teens will tell you that pleading "peer pressure" as an excuse for taking drugs is nothing more than a cop-out. It takes all the responsibility away from the user. Just saying "Billy made me do it" is easy. The user loves this excuse, and parents love it too. This excuse removes any feelings of responsibility or guilt from them, and everybody goes home a little relieved. Unfortunately, the acceptance of the peer pressure excuse may cause some neurological (actual organic brain damage) reasons for drug use to be ignored. Tragically, neurological reasons are often some of the most serious reasons for taking drugs.

Common Misunderstandings about the Role of Peers
A 1984 Search Institute study of young adolescents (fifth-through ninth-graders) and their parents shows that friends and peers do grow in importance between the fifth and ninth grades. The study goes on to say that young adolescents find each other, cling to each other, and are traumatized when they can't be with their friends.

Two erroneous conclusions are often drawn from this information: peer influence is a threat to healthy development, and children will abandon their parents as they move toward their peers.

Actually, peer relationships are necessary for the healthy development of your adolescent. It is in the crucible of these peer relationships that children teach each other a great deal about values, morality, sex roles, the control of aggression, and a host of other concerns. Peers can press each other toward growth and responsibility.

Regarding the second erroneous conclusion that children will abandon their parents as they move toward their peers, we find that young adolescents do want to become independent of their parents. This is a healthy and normal part of the maturation process. But even though peers become more influential between the fifth and the ninth grades and parents become less so, we still find that in no grade does the influence of peers outweigh the influence of parents.

When asked where they would turn for help and guidance on a variety of topics, young adolescents invariably said they would seek out their parents before they would seek out their peers. "To make my parents proud of me" is valued more than maintaining friendships.

The Complex "Why?" of Drug Addiction

If kids want their parents to be proud of them, why are they using drugs? Why do 42 percent of our nation's seniors see no risk in having five or more drinks every weekend? (*Under the Influence*, National Federation of Parents for Drug-Free Youth, 1987). And why do 26 percent of these seniors use marijuana? (*Drug Scene Update*, PRIDE, 1987)

It is up to us to discover why our kids are using and abusing drugs. We simply cannot blame it on "someone else's kids," seek a cure for the addiction, and consider the problem solved. The problem goes much deeper than the physical addiction—this is the primary issue to be addressed in this book. The whole child must be considered when dealing with a drug problem; every area of the child's life must be examined. I cannot give you simple, step-by-step answers and solutions, but I hope, in the course of the next seven chapters, to help you and your children either start down the road to recovery or steer clear of a drug-related problem.

Let's return to Johnny Alton, the young man whose story begins this chapter. Johnny is perceptually handicapped. (I will devote an entire chapter to the problems of the perceptually handicapped, but for now I mention it only to make a point.)

Before Johnny and his mother came to us, she had taken him to a medical doctor to seek help in curing his physical problem of chemical addiction. He was hospitalized for one week and sent home "cured." In less than two weeks, Johnny started using drugs again. *Why?* Why did Johnny "need" to take drugs? Nobody had bothered to ask this important question.

Johnny Alton couldn't "just say no" to drugs. It wasn't that easy. His problems go far deeper. A popular rock star who is currently in a drug treatment center noted, "I now realize that I have to find out 'why?'—why did I get on drugs in the first place? That's all part of getting better—finding out why. When I have the answer, I will then be able to say to other people, 'Look, don't do it' " ("Song," *People Weekly*, August 24, 1987, p. 95).

Finding out "why" is not easy. It involves looking at the child's medical records and talking to his teachers, minister, and friends; it involves the whole child, up to and especially including the parents. Drug problems are affected by all areas of life— emotional, psychological, spiritual, social, etc. So, you see, to get to the bottom of the problem, we must touch every area of the child's life. And it is imperative that parents get involved in the treatment program in order for that program to be effective.

Admitting Your Child Has a Drug Problem

Believe me, I understand how difficult it is for you to even admit there is a problem, let alone become involved in a treatment program. But what is more important than a healthy life for your child?

I find that parents usually follow a general pattern in coming to grips with their child's drug problem. I've seen it many times as I work with families. Parents start by simply denying the existence of the problem. This is not a conscious act of denial; their subconscious does not allow them to believe that their child could be involved. They don't want to believe it, so they don't admit the problem. They make statements like, "My child goes to church with me almost every Sunday. He absolutely could not be involved with those kids who use drugs, and he certainly doesn't use drugs himself."

It is not unusual for parents to say, "I almost wish he had a psychiatric problem, that would be easier to handle than the fact that he has gotten himself into this mess." They don't understand that they are indeed dealing with a psychiatric problem. Finally, when we develop a treatment program for their child, they soon come to realize that drug use is only the symptom of a much deeper problem.

Facing the reality of a drug problem causes pain and feelings of guilt. Many parents have said to me, "We feel so helpless. There is nothing we can do to help this kid." They suffer a loss of self-esteem, always asking, "Where did we go wrong?"

A genuine desire to help is obvious by the time this question is asked and treatment is well under way. During our counseling sessions, parents find the answers to this question and a host of other questions. They soon discover that they are not the sole reason for their child's addiction.

Coming to grips with the problem, seeking help, and becoming involved in the program always result in a stronger, more loving, and much wiser family unit. I encourage you—I urge you: If you suspect any evidence of drug use by your child, seek help immediately. The end result of such an action will be of immeasurable worth.

Finding Effective Treatment
I understand how difficult it is to find the proper kind of treatment. Unfortunately, far too many treatment centers are willing to help your child "get off drugs" without ever searching for the answer to why your child started taking drugs. Other treatment centers zero in on only one reason for drug abuse (a single diagnosis), keep your child for a measure of time, and send her home "cured." In no time, the child is back on drugs again.

This is so sad because loving, concerned parents have now wasted time and money only to see their child fall back into drugs. Effective treatment is more difficult (but not impossible) for these kids. It is more difficult because treatment of the whole child did not begin at the onset of the problem, thus giving the possibility for total dependence on drugs to become a well-established pattern. As I mentioned earlier, physical addiction to drugs occurs more rapidly in a young person than in adults, so early intervention is crucial.

Larry Schmidt, the second young man mentioned at the beginning of this chapter, is an example of a drug user who did not receive proper treatment for his addiction. Larry has a bipolar affective disorder. This means that he experiences extreme mood swings. He is either very "high" or very depressed. A bipolar affective disorder is congenital, present at birth, however, it is quite treatable. With proper prescription medication, the sufferer can lead a fairly normal life. But left undetected and untreated, the disorder wreaks havoc on a child.

Larry's problem was not diagnosed. And so, after his initial experimentation with drugs, he quickly became dependent on them just for day-to-day existence. Finding drugs was easy for Larry. In the crowd he ran with, many were selling drugs just to support their own habits. They didn't have to force Larry to use; they simply enticed him. And this was easy because Larry was a confused and hurting adolescent.

Now, Peggy Williams, the third teen whose story is cited at the beginning of this chapter, had a rather unique initial acquaintance with drugs. Her mother's innocent offer of Valium initiated a full-blown addiction. Ironically, her mother did not become addicted to Valium. Over a period of about six months, she gradually quit taking it as her physical and mental strength returned.

When Peggy began her treatment with us, we immediately initiated a program which is treating all aspects of her life, not just her physical addiction. As this book unfolds, I will tell you more about Peggy's treatment and how you can evaluate the quality of the treatment program you have chosen for your child. I will also present, in detail, some of the main reasons kids get involved with drugs. If your family is presently experiencing drug-related problems, do not despair. Drug dependency and addiction can be overcome. In my years of counseling, I have seen many families overcome their difficulties and maintain a loving, drug-free family unit. It can be done. I will also offer you some steps (preventive medicine) to take to keep your child from becoming involved in drugs. This too can be done!

Above all, do not be too hard on yourself. The very fact that you have chosen to gain insight into the problem of drug use and abuse shows that you care. Nobody is perfect. All you should expect of yourself is that you will try to do your best. And if your best doesn't seem to be good enough, the wise among you will seek outside help.

Outside help may come from many sources: church, family, friends, teachers, psychiatrists, etc. A combination of all of these will offer an abundance of aid to you in your time of need. As a matter of fact, a recent Search Institute survey of our nation's drug problem concluded:

> Chemical use, particularly alcohol, has become so commonplace and so well intrenched in American life that it seems naive to expect any single force (family, church, school, law enforcement, courts, and youth organizations) to be able to effectively intervene (*Minnesota Survey*, Search Institute, 1983, p. 104).

At our clinic, we enlist the help of every person who is involved with our patients. We offer counseling for families; we give independent psychological counseling; we do educational therapy; we prescribe the right kind of medication if medication is needed. We realize that one person cannot treat the whole child. That is precisely the reason we have a center where psychologists, psychiatrists, social workers, and special education teachers all work together. And this is the type of treatment center I urge you to seek for your child. In my opinion, it is the only way to treat children and teens.

I don't claim to have all the answers, but I do know that it takes more than one individual to treat a child who is using drugs. It takes the involvement of many loving, caring professionals to guide your child and your family back to functioning as a sound unit.

Before we move on to chapter two and attempt to ascertain just exactly what role society plays in the daily lives of our children, let's review the answers to the quiz at the beginning of the chapter. Did you find yourself changing your answers as you read the chapter?

As I said earlier, experimentation with drugs used to be relatively harmless if the child did not do it so often that it was no longer experimentation, but habit. Today, however, experimentation brings with it an ever increasing risk of severe damage and sometimes even death. Couple experimentation with the fact that the younger the child, the quicker addiction can happen, and we have an extremely dangerous situation for our children. The tremendous increase of drug experimentation over the last two decades and the alarming drop in the age of initial experimentation are of great concern to me and to all parents.

Sadly, nicotine is a "legal" drug, and more often than not there is an adult smoker somewhere in the life of every child. Even if we were to discount all the health hazards of smoking, we still have to realize that cigarette smoking can, and does, lead to use of illicit drugs.

And, parents, even though you have a kid who yells at you, one who never seems to want you within six miles of him, and one who would almost "rather die" than be seen with you, you still have a kid who loves and needs you. Ironically, the more he needs and wants your intervention, the more he growls and complains. Don't become worried if he spends hours on the phone talking to his friends (unless your phone bill gets too high). He is not rejecting you. He is beginning to exercise his natural inclination to become independent of you. He still wants your guidance and supervision. I know he seems absolutely impossible to live with, and you have to muster all the patience in the world to cope with him at times, but he loves you and respects you and, in the end, will listen to you.

If you suspect that your teen does have a drug problem, don't wait for it to get better. The chances are that it will steadily get worse. And if you cannot communicate with him in any way, call a psychologist or a psychiatrist and seek professional advice on how to approach him so that treatment can begin as soon as possible. If you don't know a professional to call, ask your school counselor or your minister to recommend someone. Get professional advice on how to approach your child and to obtain treatment for him. If your child is not using drugs, then let this book be a tool in keeping your child drug free. Drugs are everywhere. We cannot sit back and say, "My child? Never!"

Your Child's
Confusing World

Did the survey of the drug scene in the previous chapter seem a little frightening? I hope it was; I hope you'll take what I said very seriously.

Let's look now at your child's world—the environment in which he studies and socializes, his peers, and his special temptations.

First, consider some hard facts:

1. A survey reveals that 47 percent of middle-class American ninth-graders attended a party during 1986 at which alcohol was readily available.
2. In some school districts, teachers are asked to sign an affadavit which states that they will not teach moral values in the classroom.
3. Some schools in the United States teach "respon-

sible drug use."

4. Divorce is a major factor causing kids to use drugs.

5. Studies show that parents don't realize their children worry about nuclear war, national violence, and drug and alcohol abuse.

6. Studies show that an increasing number of fifth- and sixth-graders who worry about major world problems do not have the emotional and intellectual capacities to cope with these worries.

Not too long ago, a friend and I were discussing the temptations and resulting frustrations today's kids face.

"You know, Ross, I really feel sorry for my kid. I was a teen during the late fifties, and I didn't have the temptations during my entire adolescence that my son has on a daily basis.

"Our family owned one car, and we had to take turns using it. I got it one Saturday and one Sunday out of each month. If I wanted it any more often than that, I had to work out a deal with my older brother. We didn't have much of an alcohol problem, and none of my crowd used illicit drugs. Maybe it was because we didn't have all that much money. I don't know. But I do know that my Tom is sure faced with a lot of temptations."

I readily agreed with my friend. Twenty years ago, kids had nowhere near the freedom kids have today. Today almost every family has at least two cars. I'm not putting down material gain, but it does offer more mobility and freedom which create more temptations for teens.

Today's teens can always find transportation to R-rated movies full of foul language. Twenty years ago, four-letter words were practically nonexistent in movies; today, it is unheard of not to be faced with a barrage of four-letter words in any movie. Television offers a display of pornography and violence that was unimaginable just a few years ago. Our society is becoming so saturated with violence that our kids are becoming numb to it.

If you want a clear picture of how the world has changed, sit down and write ten differences between your teen years and the years of your teen. You will be greatly surprised and dismayed.

Although little objective data exists to prove it, life today is much more stressful for our children than it was for us twenty or twenty-five years ago. Our children are not at fault for the problems of today; they just happen to have been born at this time.

Current studies tell us that today's kids have different worries than kids had twenty years ago. For example, 76 percent of 1,000 kids, ages eight to seventeen, worry about the possibility of being kidnapped. Sixty-five percent of these same kids worry about the possibility of a nuclear war (*Young Adolescents and Their Parents*, Search Institute, 1984, p. 97).

And as I stated at the beginning of this chapter, most parents are not aware of their children's concerns. They think that today's kids worry more about how their friends are going to treat them than about world hunger and poverty. One study concerning peer relationships showed that only 39 percent of fifth-graders were concerned with peer relationships while 62 percent of parents felt they were concerned. On the other hand, 52 percent of those same fifth-graders were concerned about world hunger and poverty, while only 10 percent of parents realized their children had that worry.

This study concluded that the majority of the adolescents surveyed have a strong desire to communicate with their parents about these worries. Being able to talk out their worries helps adolescents to handle them (*Young Adolescents and Their Parents*, Search Institute, 1984, pp. 96, 210).

Sadly, a 1986 Search Institute study shows that our children are experiencing a growing alienation from family, school, and community.

Recent demographic surveys reveal that two thirds of American parents feel a need to be free from their children as much as possible in order to "live their own lives" (*Source*, Vol. II, No. 3, Search Institute Source, August 1986). These parents are no longer taking the responsibility for their children. And so where do these children go with their concerns and worries? With little support at home, they are left to cope in any way they can and, you guessed it, drugs can do a lot to alleviate worries, at least for the moment.

Values Society Has Neglected

According to Search Institute, today's society, with its attitudes of "individualism" and "me first," is failing miserably to impart the values of self-restraint, compassion, and commitment to our children. Every child is born with caring instincts which need to be nurtured by caring adults. This is not happening. Instead, the caring instincts of our nation's young people, centered on others and on the welfare of the wider world, fall victim to "galloping self-centered-itis."

I am saddened by Search Institute's discoveries about the values of self-restraint, compassion, and commitment. Let's look at self-restraint, for example. Those traditional and time-honored cultural values of personal conduct such as telling the truth, respecting others' property, and practicing self-control are not in evidence today. Instead, such pleasure-seeking activities as drug use and premarital sex, both of which can be harmful to self and others, are at an all-time high. One look at the rising rate of unmarried, pregnant teenagers an verify this.

And compassion which is all about caring, kindness, generosity, and working toward social justice—how evident is that in your child's world? When did you last hear of a young person who helped an ailing, elderly neighbor? Again I say, we cannot totally blame the kids—they are not being taught.

Commitment has to do with loyalty. It is a reason for living. It can be referred to as a "calling"; it gives an overall purpose and direction to life. When you ask a teen today about his future plans and why he has chosen his specific direction, does he desire a future of commitment to mankind with little mention of salary or does he simply state, "Whatever I do, it's going to be the highest paying job I can find"? (*Source*, Vol. II, No. 3, Search Institute, August 1986)

Recent studies tell us that today's teens do not consider the values of self-restraint, compassion, and commitment important. In Search Institute's 1986 study of America's young adolescents (fifth- through ninth- graders), one half of the seventh graders and two thirds of the ninth-graders report cheating on tests during the last 12 months. Eighty-eight percent of the nation's ninth-graders report lying to their parents once or more, and one third say they lied six or more times during the last 12 months.

In another survey, "three out of ten high school seniors report shoplifting, and 42 percent of ninth-grade boys report one or more incidents of vandalism, both during the last 12 months" (*Source*, Vol. II, No. 3, Search Institute, August 1986).

The list of statistics is endless. The conclusion is undeniable. Society is not encouraging a trend toward self-restraint. Rather, society is encouraging the pursuit of self-fulfillment and pleasure, both leading to use of illicit drugs.

Compassionate acts (people-helping activities) are no more obvious today than is self-restraint. Less than 10 percent of our nation's high school seniors "donate one hour or more per week to giving help to other people" (*Source*, Vol. II, No. 3, Search Institute, August, 1986). A primary goal in child rearing should be to develop a balance of giving and taking. It seems, however, that the scales are tipping toward taking, teaching our young people the false idea that life is only for pleasing and serving self. This is a very shaky premise on which to face the challenges of adulthood.

According to Search Institute, "We are seeing young people who are mimicking values that are present in society at large, embodied in social institutions (home, family, church, schools), modeled by significant adults, and forced into their daily lives by the print and broadcast media." Wherever our young people turn, they are being pressured to "be happy—be pain-free— indulge in individualism with no concern for your fellowman" (*Source*, Vol. II, No. 3, Search Institute, August 1986).

Unraveling Families
Adults are not curbing these tendencies by modeling the importance of values. Children are losing precious interaction time with their parents. Families are unraveling. Between 1960 and

1980, the population of children under 18 years of age who experienced the divorce of parents increased 140 percent (*Source*, Vol. II, No. 3, Search Institute, August 1986). Because divorce is very damaging to children, I try, whenever possible, to encourage couples who are seeking divorce to try to reconcile their differences and rebuild their marriages.

Divorce is a prime factor causing kids to use drugs. The current popular theory that children are "pliable and resilient" couldn't be further from the truth. Children are not pliable and resilient. They are extremely fragile, and no child can go through a divorce intact.

Divorce causes anger, depression, and guilt; anger, depression, and guilt cause drug abuse. A kid almost always blames himself for the divorce of his parents no matter how hard they try to explain it away. Sadly, drugs are a convenient method of numbing the child's pain over divorce.

Sometimes the child is helped by a divorce, but usually not. The child's needs should come first. When a divorce is pending, however, the needs of the child rarely enter the picture. And so the child is left floundering and often turns to drugs in frustration. Peggy Williams gives us an example of the hurt suffered by children when divorce comes into a family.

During one of our counseling sessions, sixteen-year-old Peggy sat quietly for some time before we began to talk. Finally, I said, "You seem deep in thought today, Peggy. Would you like for me to know any of those thoughts?"

"Oh, Dr. Campbell, I was just thinking about a really stupid thing I did at school. I'm afraid if I tell you, you'll think I'm awful for doing it."

"Don't worry about that, Peggy. I know you're not awful. Quite the contrary. I think you're a fine young lady."

"Well, here's what happened. One day I drove to school early and snuck a note into my locker. I wrote it, but I disguised my handwriting. The note threatened harm to me. I made sure that nobody saw me put the note in my locker, and then I went to the front door of the school and waited for my friends.

"When they got to school, I casually walked down to my

locker with them, pretending that it was the first time I had been there that morning. I made sure they saw the note sticking out of the locker door before I grabbed it and opened it. Then I read it and began to scream.

"I did this whole routine a couple more times that month, and then one night I dented in the door of my car. I wanted people to think that somebody else had done it and was trying to hurt me. My parents didn't notice the dent, but when I drove to school the next morning, the principal saw it and called my parents. My dad got all upset and demanded adult protection for me. But the principal couldn't spare any teachers or anything, so he had three of the football players walk me to and from classes and to and from the bus. My dad made me start riding the bus because of the dent in my car. I hadn't thought he'd do that, or I might have done something besides denting my car.

"Anyway, I really acted the whole thing out. Everytime I found a note, I screamed and ran to the principal's office. The principal would calm me down and promise to try to get to the bottom of it all. I even described a boy at school that I didn't like as the person I thought was leaving the notes. I thought I had everything under control, I was sure I had covered all my tracks.

"But, without me knowing it, the assistant principal started investigating my problem. He followed me a lot, but I didn't even know it. One morning when I went in to hide another note, he walked right up behind me and said, 'Give me that note, young lady.' I nearly fainted. I didn't know anybody was around.

"We had a big counseling session then. My mom and dad came to school, and the counselor and the assistant principal were there. I didn't want to listen to them, so I just told them that my two best girlfriends had dropped me and that I was trying to get their attention and make them my friends again. Everybody seemed to believe it, and I guess they all were satisfied. I know I wasn't."

"Why do you suppose you did all of that, Peggy?"

"I don't know. Just mad and hurt, I guess."

34

"At your friends?"

"No."

"Did it help you to get over being mad and hurt?"

"No."

"I wonder why you were so mad."

"A hundred things, maybe. I couldn't talk to Mom ever. She just hated for anyone to be upset. And she and Dad argued all the time. How would you feel, Dr. Campbell, if your parents told you that they were going to get a divorce and that you had to decide which one you wanted to live with?"

Peggy's sad, brown eyes filled with tears, and she covered her face with her hands.

"I'd feel mad too, Peggy. And I'll tell you what else I'd probably do—I'd probably cry."

"It was such a silly thing to do, Dr. Campbell. I think I did it just to see if they would pay some attention to me and understand that I didn't want to make a decision between them. I wanted them to know that I needed both of them. But it didn't work. I made a fool of myself. Mom kept giving me Valium so I wouldn't be upset. Then I got started using drugs. Everything went wrong. Dr. Campbell, my whole life is one big mess."

The divorce of Peggy's parents was not the total cause of her involvement with drugs; however, she had no place to turn except to friends who happened to be using drugs. This, coupled with the fact that her mother had given her Valium many times in the past, quickly led to addiction.

Again, we can readily see why Peggy and many other teens like her are using drugs. Divorce, lack of significant adults modeling important values, and temptations all create frustrations which are too difficult for teens to handle, so they turn to friends who have a "quick fix" for pain—drugs.

"Responsible" Drug Use

Another difficult experience in the lives of many of our teens is that schools are actually teaching "responsible" drug use. Yes, many voices on the national educational scene are advocating "responsible" drug use. Schools are being supplied with information for our teens which states that if teens keep their use of drugs at a responsible level, no harm will result. Can you believe it? I suppose the next thing we will be hearing is "tips for teens concerning responsible car theft" or "maintaining responsible levels of vandalism." It sounds quite ludicrous, doesn't it? "Responsible" drug use *is* being taught in our schools. In fact, the following literature is available:

● *Responsible Drug and Alcohol Use,* written by Ruth Eng and published in 1979, tells teens to use quality drugs and to sort the seeds out of their stash. It also cautions them to be sure to use clean pot-smoking paraphernalia.

● *Chocolate to Morphine: Understanding Mind-active Drugs,* written by Andrew Weil and Winifred Rosen and published in 1982, suggests that teens should question their parents about what drugs *they* use. "Maybe they will agree to give up theirs if you will give up yours. If you can convince them that your drug use is responsible, you may be able to allay their anxiety."

Weil and Rosen go on to advise parents that they should not make their children feel guilty if they get high. To quote the authors: ". . . there are no bad drugs, only bad relationships with drugs."

● *A Six Pack and a Fake I.D.* was written by Susan and David Cohen and published in 1986. They offer this counsel to teens: "If you're planning a drinking party, and your parents accept the idea, then at least try to make your party a safe, pleasant, and interesting one, instead of a drunken bash. . . . Don't overdo the amount of alcohol in the punch and don't let anyone else add to it." The Cohens, however, end their book with the following warning: "Adults who knowingly supply alcohol to minors may be liable to criminal penalties" (R.A. Hawley, "Schoolchildren and Drugs: The Fancy That Has Not Passed," *Phi Delta Kappan,* May 1987, pp. K6, K7).

With these books and others like them available in the libraries of our schools, do we really need to wonder why kids experiment with drugs? Who really knows what is going on in the private lives of these kids who are being taught responsible use of drugs. Maybe this teaching will be the impetus which leads them to a lifetime of drug abuse.

What Really Does Happen at School?

We must be ever mindful of what is going on in our schools. I'm not saying that every school has a library filled with books advocating the use of drugs. A number of good things are going on in our public schools. Conscientious students and concerned teachers are developing drug prevention and drug awareness programs. You should stay in touch with your child's teachers and other school personnel. You need to know what's *really* happening at school.

Recently a friend told me a story about the coach in his son's school. The incident does not involve drugs in a direct way, but the anger and frustration suffered by the boys involved could very easily have created an initial reason for experimentation.

My friend explained, "One evening, at a cookout, the father of our son's friend explained that the basketball coach was making our boys participate in a pink panty drill. I was shocked when this father explained that the coach conducts a free throw drill with everyone expected to get a rebound. The loser has to stand in the middle of the gym floor and put a pair of women's lace-trimmed, pink underwear on over his gym clothes and wear them during that entire practice session. Apparently, this drill has been going on ever since Coach Shoen has been at the school.

"I couldn't believe we had not heard about the drill from our son, Tim. When I asked Tim why he hadn't told us, he said, 'Oh, geez, Dad. It's no big deal. Everybody has to do it, so I just put them on and try real hard to forget I'm wearing them.'

"Shelly and I made an appointment with our principal and superintendent; we even talked to school board members on an individual basis. We requested that the drill be eliminated from future basketball practices. We were told that we were too upset over an insignificant issue, and that no one wanted to put the coach in an embarrassing light. Eventually Coach Schoen must have become uncomfortable with the whole issue because he resigned.

"Shelly and I were just sick about the whole matter. We realized that nobody was paying any attention to how the boys on the team felt. Oh, sure, the boys were saying, 'Hey, man, it's no big deal,' but what were they *really* feeling? Our Tim's words kept ringing in our ears—*'I just put them on and tried real hard to forget I was wearing them.'* If it was 'no big deal,' why was Tim trying to forget he had them on?

"Shelly and I were concerned that Tim might have some enemies among the basketball team members due to our action, but it didn't turn out that way. Almost every boy on that team came to Tim and said, essentially, 'Tim, I'm glad Schoen is gone. I hated that 'pink panty drill!' "

I couldn't believe my friend's story. I can only guess at the anger, frustration, and disappointment that these young boys felt. And I wonder what kind of advice this coach might have given any one of these boys who felt a need to go to him with a personal problem. This story stresses the point that we as parents must be totally involved in the lives of our children. I'm not advising you to follow them everywhere they go. I am saying that you should know their friends, teachers, coaches, church youth leaders, and Sunday School teachers.

Does Anyone Really Care about Morality?

Negative influences lurk in every area of your child's life. For example, I recently read an article from a very prominent girl's teen magazine. It dealt with sex under the influence of drugs and alcohol.

Ironically, the author makes a weak statement against drugs, but advises readers to be sure to have contraceptives available when planning to have responsible sex. She states: "Sex is best when you share your love with just the right person and when you choose, with a clear mind, what the two of you will do" (Kathy McCox, "Sex under the Influence: The Hazards of Drugs," *Seventeen*, Dec. 1986, p. 52). In other words, premarital sex is OK, just don't get pregnant.

Morality seems to be at an all-time low in our nation. Paul Sorvino addressed this dilemma in a recent discussion on his television show. He is obviously concerned about the lack of morality in television.

> There is something missing. There is no real moral force anymore. It's just fighting the bad guys, but there seems to be no essential goodness. I, for one, am tired of gratuitous sexuality and violence. The acquisition of wisdom is an idea that is bankrupt. Nobody believes in such a thing. People believe in acquisition, but not for knowledge—not for truth. We have become acquisitive for power, but not for love—not for honor. Where are all these things? (Kenneth R. Clark, "Sorvino Wants Return of Morality," *St. Louis Dispatch*, Oct. 23, 1987, p. 11H)

Columnist Bob Greene recently interviewed a sixteen-year-old Alabama girl who is a member of the National Honor Society at her school. She had just read an essay about people's reactions to the assassination of John F. Kennedy on November 22, 1963.

She explained to Greene, "Your generation lost its innocence on November 22, 1963. My generation has no innocence to lose. And if what my generation has now is innocence, I shudder to think what our version of November 22, 1963 will be. I am 16 years old now and I expect to see another president die at the hands of an assassin in my lifetime. Some innocence, huh?"

She went on to explain how she thinks the world has changed: "Today I think of kids working after school and at nights so that they can give money to their moms because their dads have left home. I think of kids being concerned mainly about things like being busted for going into a bar underage. The idea of fourth-graders being confronted with drugs. Think back to when you [Greene] were in the fourth grade. Can you imagine a kid coming to school stoned or drunk? . . .

"It's just that we've become so jaded so early. Everybody's seen everything by the time they're 15 or 16. You can turn on cable TV and see people in bed together. I was watching a movie on cable TV, and even the donkey was snorting cocaine. . . .

"Sometimes I wonder: When I look back on being a kid, what will I think?" (Bob Greene, "Innocence Lost," *Austin American-Statesman*, Nov. 4, 1987, p. C5)

Quite a sad statement from a very astute and mature sixteen-year-old.

Somebody Forgot to Raise the Children

Possibly this young lady, with millions of other young people, is coming home from school to an empty house and a single parent family. My experience has taught me that divorce and the world that is created by parents who are needing self-fulfillment produces a by-product of lonely children who are prime candidates for experimentation with drugs—experimentation which so often leads to dependence and addiction.

Here I want to stress that I am *not* against women's rights; I am *not* against civil rights; I am *not* against anybody's rights, but I am seeing that somewhere along the way, somebody forgot to raise the children.

I am afraid that society is failing its children. It is up to us as loving, responsible parents to pick up the pieces and create a better world for our kids. Our children may appear to be strong and unbreakable, but in fact they are fragile beings.

Our children need constants in their daily lives. They want us to set down rules. They have an innate need to be loved unconditionally. They need to know ethical and moral values, as taught in Christianity, in order to develop as whole beings. Parents, your children need you and want you in their lives. For example, remember Tim, whose coach put women's underwear on him? He was proud that his parents intervened. Their actions told Tim that he was important.

Children are not equipped to really defend themselves. To a large degree, they are victims of circumstances created by the older generation. They give us joy. They evoke our tears. They give us reason to hope. They demand responsible care from us. They are the children God has given us. We must not fail them.

I started using drugs when I entered junior high. I smoked marijuana, but soon it didn't do the job anymore. Then I was introduced to cocaine. From the first time I used it, cocaine was my first and last love.

Matt, age 17, drug addict

Anger
and Drugs

Now that you have an overall view of the frustrations and temptations your children face, you are better equipped to understand why they may become angry and use drugs to cope with their confusing world.

Before we begin our discussion about anger as a cause of drug use and abuse, check you response to the following statements.

Yes   No

1. My child yells and verbalizes his frustrations only on rare occasions.
2. My child rarely argues with his siblings.
3. My child is quiet and works constantly to keep peace among his siblings.

4. My child never seems to have a problem, but all of his friends come to him with their problems.
5. My child does everything we tell him to do with little argument.
6. It is obvious that my child tries very hard to please both his parents.
7. My child seems concerned when his grades go down, but he does not talk to me about it.
8. My child never talks with me about his worries.
9. My friends often compliment me on the behavior and manners of my child.
10. I am pleased that my child does not disrupt our household with outbursts of anger.
11. Anger is an unnecessary emotion. It only serves to disrupt our family.
12. Anger has little to do with drug use.

Hopefully you were able to answer no to the majority of these questions. If you answered yes to more than half of them, I urge you to work on communicating with your child and helping him learn to express his anger. (I will give you some tips in this chapter.)

Anger Is a Normal Emotion

Webster's New World Dictionary tells us that anger is a feeling of displeasure resulting from injury, mistreatment, opposition, etc. Now, let's apply that definition to our daily lives. Have you ever stubbed your toe and yelled? When you did, maybe you yelled because of the injury or insult to your foot and then felt somewhat better. Right?

But what happens at your house when your child comes home from school in a bad mood and starts growling for no apparent reason? Do you let him growl and help him to arrive at the real cause of his anger and frustration so that he can feel somewhat better? If you're like most parents, and we've all certainly done is many times, you send him to his room until he can settle down.

What we must realize is that anger is a normal emotion, and it must be expressed just like any other emotion. I am suggesting to you that you try a different approach the very next time your child comes home "in a huff."

Let's say that your son, Tom, just came through the kitchen door.

"Hi, Tom. Did you run all your errands?"

"Mom, do you have to ask me every little thing I do? I wish you'd just leave me alone once in a while. Where's Dad?"

"I don't know where he went, Tom, but he should be back in a few minutes because he and I are going shopping this afternoon."

"Honestly, Mom. Is that all you can do? Just think of ways to spend money?"

By this time you are ready to dismiss Tom to his room and maybe even threaten to keep the car from him for a week. But you don't. Instead, you say, "Tom, you're obviously angry about something. Let's try to figure out what it is. We both know that I'm not a nosy mother, and I can find plenty of things to do that don't require spending money."

Tom probably won't sit right down and spill all his troubles but before the evening is over, the chances are good that he will come to you and say something like "Mom, I got a warning ticket when I was running errands. I was afraid Dad would be pretty disgusted about it."

Tom probably won't apologize in a straightforward way, but he may mention that his outburst really wasn't because of anything you did.

Handling Tom's anger in this manner has allowed him to "blow off a little steam" and still get to the source of the problem. If he had been sent to his room immediately, his anger would have been kept inside him, which can eventually be damaging. Anger is normal. It is only when an expression of anger becomes physically harmful that strong measures must be taken to handle the situation.

Children must be taught that feeling and expressing anger is normal. We must help them learn to express those feelings in a mature, positive manner by placing the blame where it belongs and discussing the problem. This method of handling anger takes time and practice, but it can be done.

Parents Must Understand Their Own Anger

In teaching their children to express anger in a mature way, I encourage parents to first look at their own methods of dealing with anger. Many times, kids are simply copying the parental example set before them.

Let me tell you about Greg and Carol Wassel. They had come to me because their son, Andrew, had been caught smoking pot. After a number of counseling sessions with Andrew and his family, we discovered that Andrew's drug use was a result of not being able to express his anger appropriately.

On their initial visit, the Wassels sat in my office, obviously nervous, but anxious to tell me all about Andrew.

"I'll tell you what, Dr. Campbell, that Andrew is about to become a no-good," Greg Wassel began. "I've never seen such an unappreciative kid in my life. Why, when I was his age, if I had been given half the opportunities he has, I would have run with them. But what does this kid do—he runs off and smokes dope with a bunch of pot-heads. I can't see it. I told Carol that what that boy really needs is a taste of my belt."

"Now, Greg," Carol interrupted, "Andrew hasn't always been defiant, and we only know of this one incident of him smoking pot. Why don't we ask Dr. Campbell if he can give us some insight into this whole thing. I don't think Andrew is a bad boy. Something has gone wrong for him."

"Why don't you let me talk with all of you on an individual basis, and then we can all get together and go to work on this problem," I suggested. "It is easier for me to help a family if I can learn about each of the personalities in this manner."

During the counseling sessions, as I talked with each of the family members, I quickly learned that Greg was a very angry man and that Andrew was receiving all of this displaced anger. As soon as Greg began to realize that the true source of his anger was concern about his job, he could see what he was doing to Andrew.

It is easy to understand that when parents become tired or worried, a teenager's actions can quickly create tension and provoke anger. Often, all of the parental anger is dumped on the teenager, not just the anger specifically caused by the teen's actions. This is extremely detrimental. Nothing cuts off communication between a parent and an adolescent the way poorly controlled parental anger does.

I made a number of suggestions to Greg and Carol about learning to deal with their own anger. I suggested that they each try to find some time during each day that they could be alone. In these moments alone I encouraged them to do things such as thinking positive thoughts or listening to pleasant music to relieve their minds of tension. I also suggested that they watch the foods they eat because maintaining a healthy physical condition can reduce irritability.

"But Dr. Campbell," Greg interrupted, "even if we do all these things, isn't it still normal to get mad once in awhile?"

"Of course it is, Greg. It's just that when you can understand the source of your anger and even apologize to your teen when you overreact, you are well on the road to handling anger in a mature, positive manner. Then you will be able to teach your child how to express his anger."

Teaching Your Child to Express Anger Appropriately

As I talked with the Wassels, they began to understand that Greg's worries were causing him to overreact with Andrew, thus creating a very negative relationship between them. "Now, I have some suggestions for helping Andrew with his anger. But I want to talk with all of you together about this."

Andrew wasn't happy about talking to me with his parents present. He was obviously uncomfortable in his father's presence. But as our sessions progressed, he let his guard down somewhat.

"Do you ever get angry enough to throw something, Andrew?" I asked.

"Yes, I did that once, but I really caught it from Dad."

"You caught it from me because you broke that mirror I had gotten your mother for her birthday," Greg Wassel interrupted.

"I'll tell you what Andrew—I have some suggestions about learning to express anger. I have here a list of ways people express their anger. Let's read it together and try to find where you are on this list."

I pointed out the five steps at the top of the list:

Thinking logically and constructively
Holding to the primary complaint
Focusing anger on source only
Seeking resolution
Pleasant behavior

I explained that these steps suggest the most desired way to deal with anger. The angry person should learn to think logically and constructively, progress through the other steps, and eventually arrive at pleasant behavior. Next, I directed the Wassels to the bottom of the list:

Unpleasant and loud behavior
Cursing
Displacing anger to sources other than the original
Expressing unrelated complaints
Throwing objects
Destroying property
Verbal abuse
Emotionally destructive behavior
Physical abuse
Passive-aggressive behavior

I explained how passive-aggressive behavior is the poorest way to express anger. Physical abuse is another extremely poor expression of anger. Emotionally destructive behavior, an uncontrolled release of strong feeling demonstrated by destroying property or inflicting pain, is only one step above physical abuse. Throwing objects, unpleasant and loud behavior, and other behaviors at the bottom of the list show improvement in ways of expressing anger, but they are still far from ideal behavior.

"What do you think?" I questioned Andrew.

"Well," he began, "I don't hit people when I get mad, and I haven't been destroying property, except for Mom's mirror, but I do throw things now and then. But I don't understand this. Am I supposed to never get mad again? I don't think I can do that."

"Of course not, Andrew. All fourteen-year-old boys become angry. As a matter of fact, anger is quite normal. But throwing things is not a healthy way of expressing that normal anger. So we are going to work on learning how to express anger in a mature, positive manner. We won't get it all done today, but I am pleased to see that all of you are interested and eager to solve your problems, so this shouldn't take too long."

"Andrew is a good boy, Dr. Campbell. I think he's come a long way already, and I think we'll get the rest of this figured out," his mother said.

And I think they will. The Wassels are a loving family who got off on the wrong track for a while but are working to correct their situation. I urged them to encourage Andrew to express anger and keep track of where he is on the anger ladder. I suggested that they praise Andrew for expressing his anger and then talk to him about one of the inappropriate ways he may be using (for example, throwing objects) and begin to correct this.

"Above all," I stressed, "try to be patient. Keep in mind that anger is normal and expect Andrew to progress one step at a time. An unfortunate expectation of parents is that their children will handle anger maturely, with no training. We all know that this is impossible. Remember too that your child's personality has a great deal to do with how he handles his anger."

Suppressed Anger and Drug Abuse

As we have seen in this discussion of the Wassels, anger can cause some serious problems. His father's displaced anger caused such resentment in Andrew that he withdrew from the family.

He not only became a behavioral problem at home, but he also began to experiment with drugs. I am so glad that Andrew's parents brought him to me before he began to suppress his anger. This can and often does lead to very serious problems for the teen.

Anger, when it is constantly suppressed, is one of the major causes of drug abuse. Since angry kids want to get back at authority figures, and authority figures stress that drugs should not be used, what is the first thing an angry kid is going to do? Yes, he is going to experiment with drugs. More often than not, the child himself does not realize that he is using drugs to get back at anybody.

The primary cause of anger in most children is that they are not having their emotional needs met. A child must feel loved and receive love from his parents or his primary caretaker in order to develop normally. Constant denial of love and attention is extremely detrimental to any child. And drugs are a convenient way for an unloved child to ease his pain and anger.

Children who live in single parent homes or homes where two parents are working are prone to anger. Simple logic explains the reason—these parents have so little time to show their children affection. When both parents have to work, they have to do double duty at home to develop a loving, stable environment for their children. Finding the time to make your children feel your love for them is certainly not impossible, but it does require careful management. It is of utmost importance.

Children so easily feel that an absent parent means a lack of love. They instinctively feel this at a very early age. Let's take, for example, a toddler whose parents have left her for a weekend. When they return, the child does not reach eagerly for them but remains for a while in the arms of the sitter. It seems improbable that a child of eighteen months would feel anger toward her parents, but that is exactly what happens. The toddler is angry. She has been denied the love and attention of her parents for one entire weekend. Many children of working parents or divorced parents also equate the absence of a parent or parents with a lack of love, and these feelings of being unloved result in anger. I don't know of anything more important to your children than unconditional love; it goes a long way in helping them through all of their growing-up years.

I stress here that even the most loved child still feels anger. As I said earlier, anger is a normal, usually healthy emotion. So don't feel that you have failed your toddler, child, or teen when he expresses anger. Just be sure that he does express his anger so that it does not remain bottled up inside him and finally come out as passive-aggressive behavior when he becomes an adult.

Passive-aggressive Behavior

I have dealt at length with anger and passive-aggressive behavior in chapter seven of an earlier book entitled *How to Really Love Your Teenager* (Victor), but I must mention it here in order to show the relationship between anger and drugs.

Passive-aggressive behavior is suppressed anger that unconsciously comes out from a child or an adult in negative behavior. Some examples of passive-aggressive behavior are: tardiness, pouting, forgetting, stubbornness, or intentional inefficiency. Passive-aggressive individuals resent rules and manage not to comply with demands others make of them. Resentment against authority figures is very apparent in passive-aggressive personalities.

Passive-aggressive behavior is normal in only one period of time in an individual's life, and that is the adolescent years, ages twelve or thirteen through sixteen or seventeen. Did you happen to notice the change in your child near his thirteenth birthday? Did you notice that he became very intelligent (in his own estimation) and that you became quite ignorant (again, according to his judgment)? He began to exhibit anger for no apparent reason and "No!" constituted his vast vocabulary. Don't worry. He became an adolescent. He is beginning to break away from the nest and is undergoing many frustrating and sometimes devastating experiences.

It is advisable for you to devise methods of letting your child express his passive-aggressive behavior in ways that are not harmful. For example, what teen do you know who has a clean room? Keeping a messy room is simply an example of passive-aggressive behavior. If a child is raised right, he is going to choose innocuous ways to express his passive-aggressive behavior, such as, wearing socks with holes in them, using sloppy eating habits, or not cleaning his room.

You tell your child you want a clean room, and she gives you a sloppy room. Wonderful! You are keeping the passive-aggressive behavior confined to your child's own bedroom. Isn't it much easier to live with a messy room than to work with a child who uses drugs?

You must bear in mind that you can't totally prevent passive-aggressive behavior. It is primarily unconscious, and the unconscious mind is amoral (not immoral). It sees neither right nor wrong. It senses the normal emotion of anger and knows the emotion must come out. If allowed to express his anger verbally, and taught how to handle his anger in a mature way, your child will finally develop into a strong adult. All of you will come through the passive-aggressive stage intact.

Excessive suppressed anger will cause passive-aggressive behavior to last long beyond its normal period, probably throughout the life of the individual. So you can readily see why anger must be expressed and handled in a positive way.

Angry Johnny Alton and Peggy Williams
Johnny Alton is a prime example of a kid who is extremely angry, and his drug use is a direct result of that anger. Both his parents love him, but his mother has been so involved in coping with the problems of living with an alcoholic husband that she rarely shows Johnny any love. And his father is having such a struggle with his own addiction that he spends little time with Johnny.

When Johnny first came to see me, his anger was obvious. He did not want to talk. "I don't know what I'm doin' here," he complained. "My old man needs this worse than I do."

"Well, maybe he'll come in sometime, and we'll get acquainted," I suggested.

"Don't count on it," Johnny spit sarcastically. "I've never been able to depend on him, so I don't know why you should think you can."

"How do you and your father get along, Johnny?"

"I'll tell you, Dr. Campbell. The only time he speaks to me is when he's runnin' low on booze and he accuses me of drinkin' it. Listen, man, I don't drink. I can find stuff better than that to get high on.

"I tell him he's nuts and he knows it! And then my mom starts yellin' at us. And she accuses me too. I wonder if she'll ever get smart."

"What do you mean by that, Johnny?"

"I mean, I wonder if she'll ever get smart and realize that my old man is an alcoholic. I think she knows it, she just don't want to admit it. It's easier to blame me for things 'cause I won't hit her. My old man has slapped her around a couple of times."

"I'm sorry to hear that, Johnny. That must be very painful for you."

"Naw, I just bug out and smoke a few joints with my friends. My folks are usually both in bed and asleep by the time I come home."

The source of Johnny's anger is all too obvious. He has another source of anger, however, he is perceptually handicapped. So even if both his parents were showing him normal love, he would have difficulty perceiving it. Johnny is not retarded. He simply does not perceive the written word. The name of his particular problem is dyslexia. This problem manifests itself as the inability to read well enough to use reading as a tool for learning. Letters are sometimes reversed; whole words are sometimes scrambled beyond comprehension.

So you can readily imagine what an average school day would be like for Johnny. Add to this the fact that he goes home each day to an alcoholic father, and you can easily see why he got involved with drugs. They made him "feel good." No other area of his life feels good to him.

Johnny comes to our clinic once a week. Occasionally his mother comes with him. They are working hard toward a solution to Johnny's problems, but they still have a way to go.

Peggy Williams is a different story. She has always known that her mother loves her, but she has never been allowed the normal expression of anger that every person, especially an adolescent, must have. Every time she tried to discuss her anger about a particularly difficult or frustrating problem with her mother, she was handed a Valium and told to "try to settle down."

One day she was sitting across from me in my office in a rather pensive mood when she suddenly looked up and said, "You know, Dr. Campbell, I don't think I've ever been allowed to get mad and yell and scream. My friends have done it. When they tell me how they have argued with their mothers, I can't believe my ears. If I start any kind of really deep conversation with my mother, or if I dare get mad and try to argue with her, she simply changes the subject or tells me it's wrong to argue. Is it really wrong to argue, Dr. Campbell?"

"What do you think, Peggy? Do you ever argue with your friends and finally agree on a point or two?"

"Yeah, I've argued during class meetings about certain things I think our class should do, but we don't usually get real mad at each other. And my girlfriend and I got into an argument the other day about some shoes, but we got over it. It felt kinda good to say what I felt. I sure wish Mom understood that. She must have been some kind of perfect kid. The way she hates to argue, I'll bet she never had a fight with anybody in her life. Maybe that's why my dad left us. Mom never got mad at him. She was never able to talk to him—she was just sorta there."

"Peggy, do you realize that your use of drugs is an expression of anger toward your mother?"

"Oh, no, Dr. Campbell. I try never to get mad at her. I think it would do her in."

"I know that, Peggy. I know that you don't argue with your mother or yell at her, but deep down inside, without you even realizing it, you feel anger toward your mother and so you use drugs just to get back at her."

"Then it's sorta like a subconscious thing, huh? You mean I know it won't do any good to try to tell her when I get really mad, so I do drugs just to get back at her? Wow, I never thought of it that way."

"That's one reason, Peggy. There are other reasons for your use of drugs, but you are beginning to understand the primary reason."

I was pleased to see that Peggy was beginning to understand her relationship with her mother. I knew that we still had a long way to go, but things were beginning to take shape.

Personality Types and Drug Use

Peggy Williams is what I call a 25 percenter. Throughout my years of working with children, I have found it very helpful to categorize them in terms of how they respond to authority. I discussed this thoroughly in my book *How to Really Know Your Child* (Victor); however, a brief explanation here will help you understand your child's anger. My experience has taught me that 75 percent of us respond to authority with: "Get out of my way world, I have a life to live, and I don't need anybody telling me how to do it!" And 25 percent of us respond with: "Whatever you say, I'll try my very best to do." There are varying degrees of these attitudes present in every individual, but generally speaking, I find it extremely helpful to group people under these two headings.

Johnny Alton is a 75 percenter. No matter what his parents or his teachers say to him, he is going to do things his way. Peggy, on the other hand, wants nothing more than to please her mother, her friends, her teachers, and anyone else in her life.

It is very critical in the development of your child for you to become aware of what type of personality he has and then work with him accordingly. Seventy-five percenters seldom have trouble expressing their anger, so they must be encouraged and trained to handle it in a mature, positive way.

Twenty-five percenters go to extremes to keep peace. Although it would seem that the 75 percenter is the more difficult child of the two to raise, just the opposite is true. Twenty-five percenters may seem quiet and free of anger, but they are holding in all their anger which, as I stated earlier, is damaging. Twenty-five percenters do not express their anger because they do not want to cause trouble; therefore, the problem which arises in working with 25 percenters is that their need to express anger can be overlooked by parents. These kids seem such a joy to be with that parents fail to realize 25 percenters also feel anger and frustrations and need to express them and learn to handle them maturely.

Both personality types can experience depression resulting from suppressed anger, but it seems to be more of a problem for the 25 percenter. Please understand that neither personality trait is all bad or all good; both traits simply exist. The 75 percenter needs help in expressing anger in a positive way, and the 25 percenter needs encouragement in expressing anger, not suppressing it. I know many wonderful people who are strong 75 percenters, and I know equally as many people who are strong 25 percenters.

As a matter of fact, we have a 75 percenter and a 25 percenter at our house. Our son, David, is a true 75 percenter. David is a wonderful young man. He is a sophomore in college and is doing quite well. We are very proud of him, as we are of all our children.

My wife, Pat, and I were aware almost from the moment David was born that he was a 75 percenter. He has always had that "I'd rather do it myself!" attitude. He has always been able to express his anger without any help from us. And we have always tried to be mindful not to suppress his anger but to help him handle it in a positive, mature way.

Now Dale, on the other hand, is our 25 percenter. He has always been a very agreeable kid. Pat and I have had to be constantly on guard to make sure that Dale expresses his anger. When we notice that he is unusually quiet, we try to draw him into a conversation which will result in his telling us whether or not he is troubled.

Keep in mind that every time your child is quiet you do not have to worry that he is troubled. Most parents can usually tell the difference and act accordingly. Again I say, it is just as critical in the development of the 25 percenter as it is in the 75 percenter that he be allowed to express his anger, but of course, we must train him to handle it more and more maturely as he grows older.

Now don't feel that just because you have a 25 percenter, she is going to become severely depressed and attempt suicide, but the following is an example of what can happen when a child is never allowed to express any anger.

Joann is a sixteen-year-old, petite, well-mannered girl. She is also a typical, angry, depressed, extreme 25 percenter.

"I feel so guilty when I can't live up to the expectations of my parents," she said one day as she sat curled up in a chair in my office. "You see, Dr. Campbell, I think I have always felt that making others happy is much more important than making myself happy. And I still think that way. It is so much easier to keep everybody calmed down than it is to argue."

"Is it really, Joann?" I interrupted. "Right now you are an unhappy person. Aren't you just as important as anyone else?"

"Well, I suppose so, but you don't know my mother and daddy. It was always easier to try to please them than to buck them. For instance, I've always been kinda good at gymnastics, but I didn't place first in my last meet. After the competition, my daddy began to tell me where I went wrong, and instead of telling him that I simply didn't feel up to par, I felt guilty that I had let him down and promised him I would do better. It's always been like that. But I don't care anymore. I don't care if I never please anyone again.

"Do you know that my mother never gets mad? She has told me ever since I can remember that expressing anger is very unladylike. And so, I guess to please her, I don't get mad. At least I don't get mad on the outside. But I feel mad on the inside and guilty about it at the same time. Am I making any sense, Dr. Campbell?"

"Sure you are, Joann. I can understand how frustrated you must have been."

"Oh, I don't know if you can or not. I don't know if anyone can really understand. See, I finally gave up, I guess. But then, that's why I'm here. But you already know that. You already know that I tried suicide. You must really think I'm stupid."

No, I didn't think that Joann was stupid. I knew that she was hurting and that we were going to do all we could to help her and her family get through this. Not only had she attempted suicide, but she had also become involved in drugs.

As I stated earlier in this chapter, anger is a prime cause of drug abuse. Suppressed anger results in passive-aggressive behavior and passive-aggressive behavior is anti-everything. And since using drugs is antiauthority, kids who are not handling their anger well are prone to use drugs. Drugs can also be a form of self-medication; drugs make the anger and pain go away.

Angelo's Suppressed Anger

Sixteen-year-old Angelo sat quietly with an attitude of the perfect gentleman, but his clothes and his unkempt, long, dirty hair betrayed him. His physical appearance was a blatant act against authority. His black eyes snapped with anger. His feigned manners were, had the situation not been so serious, almost comical.

"Hello, Angelo. And how are you today?" I began on his first visit to my office.

"I'm very fine, thank you, sir," he answered in his "Sunday best" manner of speaking.

He smiled. I could see that getting a conversation started with him was going to be interesting. I looked down at his records and pretended to read them, but I was only using this action as an excuse to remain silent. He began to squirm a little. He obviously did not want to be in my office. Finally, he broke the silence.

"Are you reading something on that paper that will help me get this over with? I don't really see any reason to be here."

"Let's see, Angelo. It says here that you have been hospitalized twice due to an overdose of drugs. Is that correct?"

"Yeah, but I'm over that now."

"When your mother made this appointment, she said that you

were willing to talk with someone concerning the fact that you use drugs. Was she telling the truth?"

"Yeah, well, you gotta say a lot of things to keep her off your back."

"Like what, Angelo?"

"Like, you gotta act real nice and polite to the old lady across the street 'cause if you don't, I swear, my mom will knock your head off. Man, does she get mad, but she'll half kill you if you get mad. And you absolutely have to go to church with her every Sunday. If you dare say you don't want to, she sits down and cries and tells you all about how she is trying so hard to make a good boy out of you and all that stuff. It's just easier to go with her than put up with all of that."

"Is going to church all that bad?"

"It didn't used to be, but once in a while, I want to do what I want to do on Sunday morning, like sleep in. She gets to carryin' on something awful, tellin' me that God is going to punish me and that kind of junk. I thought God was, well, a good guy, you know what I mean? But my mom can sure change your mind. She can scare you half to death of Him. And she never lets me tell my side of anything. She can hang a guilt trip on you a mile long if you dare open your mouth and complain about anything.

"Hangin' around the house is the pits, so I do my chores and split every chance I get."

"How old were you when you started using drugs, Angelo?"

"About eleven or twelve, I guess. A couple of the guys who hung around the basketball court always had an extra joint or two, and they let me try one. It wasn't any big deal. I felt like a big shot doing it, so I kept doing it.

"Finally, it just got to be a habit. No big deal. As long as my mom thought I was being a 'good little boy' and playing a nice, respectable Saturday afternoon game of basketball, she was happy. And I figured what she didn't know wouldn't hurt her, so I kept it up. That overdose wasn't on purpose. Somebody slipped me some bad stuff."

Angelo had lost his air of feigned manners and was beginning to open up. "What about the second overdose, Angelo?"

"I don't know. Guess I was just trying to be smart and mixed some stuff. It was a bad trip."

Angelo is another kid whose parents tried to keep from showing or exhibiting anger. Through Angelo, we can see how damaging the suppression of anger can be. Anger is going to come out. It is just a matter of time and circumstance.

Allowing Verbal Expression of Anger Is Not Permissiveness

Trying to teach parents the importance of handling their child's anger properly is probably my most difficult task. When I try to explain that our children must be trained to handle their anger maturely and that this cannot be done if a young person is prohibited from verbally expressing his anger, many people disagree with me. Often people feel that allowing verbal expression of anger is a form of permissiveness which condones yelling, screaming, and other immature forms of behavior. Of course, this would be true if we could not also train our child to handle behavior more maturely in the future. (This is discussed in more detail in chapters six and seven of my book, *How to Really Love Your Teenager*.)

Another misunderstanding people often express about my approach to anger is that I am advocating a physical release of anger such as hitting and throwing. Heavens, no! Just the opposite is true. Have you noticed that I keep emphasizing the importance of encouraging the *verbal* expressions of anger, not the physical. Physical expressions of anger are inappropriate and should be handled as such. (Refer to the list of ways to deal with anger which I mentioned earlier in this chapter.)

Today's kids are bombarded with situations that create anger. Divorce is at an all-time high; schools can present some frustrating situations; physical and sexual abuse is on the increase. Anger-causing circumstances are everywhere. This fact emphasizes the need for parents to understand and use appropriate methods to deal with this anger.

Television, newspaper, and magazine advertising fairly scream with the message that everybody should feel good—

nobody should suffer pain and anger. The effects of such advertising are obvious. Kids turn to drugs because they want to "feel good."

Is it any wonder?

I would like for you to go back to the beginning of this chapter, now, and reread the test. Keep each of your children in mind as you answer the questions. Also check to see where they fit under the two general categories of 25 percenters and 75 percenters.

After reading the test for the second time, question your own feelings about anger. Are you like Joann's parents or Angelo's mother? Do you stress that your children hold their anger back? Maybe a reassessment about how anger is dealt with in your home is in order at this time. If you do make some changes, please do not expect miracle results overnight. You've been doing things one way for a long time, so it will take awhile to see the results of any changes you might make.

My baby was born at six months and lived only a few hours. I feel so guilty I could die. If I hadn't been doin' drugs, she might be alive today. Some days I feel so bad I think about committin' suicide. I want my baby.

Maureen, age 16, drug addict

Depression and Drugs

Let's move on to a discussion of depression, which goes hand in hand with anger in leading to drug abuse. Here are some facts which you need to know about childhood depression before we get into further discussion.

1. Professionals who are treating children and teens are observing an increase in childhood and teenage depression.
2. Adult depression is obvious just by looking at the depressed person, but childhood depression is very difficult to detect based on physical appearance.
3. The underlying causes of depression are very complex, but physical and sexual abuse are two major causes of depression in children and teens.

4. Depression usually will not "simply run its course."
5. A depressed and angry child is prone to drug abuse.

These facts will become clearer as we move ahead. Let's discuss the last statement first.

A short time before we started working on this book, I had lunch with a friend who is a pediatrician in our area.

"You know, Ross," he began, "sometimes I think I should hang out my shingle lettered *Grandfather on Duty, Will Listen.*"

"Hey, now you're getting into my territory." I laughed.

"I know, Ross, but many of my patients turn out to be the parents instead of the child. Let me give you an example. Just yesterday a twenty-six-year-old mother of a ten-year-old girl came in. The child had been complaining of headaches and stomachaches. I asked when these symptoms started.

"She said they seem to have started just after her husband left them, about ten months ago. She couldn't bring the child in earlier because she works full-time during the day and also keeps a part-time job at a restaurant three nights a week. She doesn't have a sitter who could have brought the child in earlier.

"Ross, I soon found myself listening to the mother's problems and realized that she needed as much if not more help than her daughter. She has no support system. The child's father offers them no monetary support, so the mother is totally on her own.

"As I concluded my examination of the child, I felt sure that the problem was depression, but I ordered some standard tests to rule out any possible physical problems. Then I suggested to the mother that she and her daughter seek counseling.

"I feel so inadequate at times, Ross. You can see why I feel the need to be an understanding grandfather figure to some of my patients, but I absolutely do not have the time.

"And my colleagues are seeing this too. Even in two-parent families, we are seeing a rise in the number of children who are ultimately diagnosed as depressed."

"I am seeing it too," I agreed. "Why do you think it is on the increase?"

"I'll tell you, Ross, I think it's because life has become so fragmented that parents don't have the time they need to spend with their kids. As a consequence, they become frustrated with their role as parents, and they try to pull out of that role.

"They begin to become involved in activities outside the home which, obviously, leaves little time for the child. All of this produces anger and resentment in the child which culminates far too often in depression. We are seeing an unusually large number of children, and I'm talking about eight-, nine-, and ten-year-olds, who complain of such vague symptoms as headaches, stomachaches, and chest pains. After a thorough physical examination, we diagnose depression.

"We're not seeing any particular class of kids with these problems—they come from the wealthiest and the poorest of families. But one thing we are noticing is that a number of our depressed children are those who have been given a tremendous amount of freedom.

"For example, we are finding that kids are left to shift for themselves at entirely too early an age. They are being forced into adult roles when they are not really ready for them. Take the little ten-year-old I was telling you about. She comes home from school each day to an empty house and is expected to do a certain amount of household chores and start supper before she starts her homework."

Lack of Unconditional Love Fosters Depression

As I drove back to my office that afternoon, our conversation stayed in my mind. My friend was seeing the same problems that we are seeing—a marked increase in childhood depression. And he is seeing the same reason for this depression. Primarily, depression in children is caused by the breakdown of the family unit.

I can't stress enough the importance of love in the life of a child—unconditional love of the whole child. Sadly, families today spend little time fulfilling that basic human need of unconditional love. The result is an angry child, and anger leads to depression. Easily available illicit drugs bring quick relief from the pain these angry and depressed kids experience daily. No wonder they are drawn to drugs.

Many professionals who treat drug and alcohol addiction blame the drugs and alcohol for the depression. To a certain extent this is true, but far too often professionals fail to see that most kids who use drugs are already depressed due to not having their basic emotional needs met. Usually, depression leads to drugs. Any negative experience of life coupled with the use of drugs and alcohol just increases the depression.

It is essential in understanding depression to be aware of the fact that the depressed child is an angry child. And it follows that the more angry the child becomes, the more depressed he becomes. The way to prevent childhood depression is nurturance. A child who is loved unconditionally will thrive in every area of his life, whereas an unloved child suffers the pain of anger and depression.

Other Causes of Adolescent Depression

Depression can be mild and relatively easy to cure, or it can be severe. An extremely severe bout with depression often results when emotional, physical, or sexual abuse has occurred. As I noted earlier, these kinds of abuse are steadily increasing. Adolescents who have been subjected to abuse not only become depressed, but they may also attempt suicide, become involved in prostitution, or become heavily involved with drugs. The pain they suffer is catastrophic. They also develop feelings of worthlessness.

A patient of mine, Tami, had spent two weeks away from home when her mother finally brought her to us.

"Well, Tami, things aren't going so well, huh? Is there any particular thing you'd like to talk about?"

"I guess I'm just a mess," she said, staring at the floor. "I've screwed up my life and everybody's around me. What can I say?" Tami never used eye contact during our conversation that first day.

It took a number of sessions, but Tami finally discussed the real reason she had run away from home. "It's not something I want to talk about, but you might as well know it—but you can't tell my mom. She'll just die. See, this guy she married last summer has been—he tries to—he keeps wanting to have sex with me." She sighed and lowered her eyes.

"Did you have sex with him, Tami?"

"Yes, he wouldn't leave me alone, so I gave in to him. Then I just got tired of the whole mess, so I ran away."

Tami's healing process will take time. She has been deeply scarred, and the pain and anger that she has suffered will take a long time to heal. She has started back to school, and we are working with her school adviser plus her medical doctor. She has had some health problems due to an abortion. And so you can see how crucial it is to check into every area of a child's life. Tami's drug addiction was truly the tip of an entire iceberg of problems.

Valerie, A Depressed 25 Percenter

At this point, I want to talk to you about the 25 percenter, depression, and drug use. As you recall, the 25 percenter is a person who desires peace and tries to please everyone.

Valerie, a rather short, stocky seventeen-year-old, came to see us after a suicide attempt. Before her initial visit, I had obtained the release of her school records and her medical records. According to her medical records, she appeared to be a physically healthy young woman.

Her school records told me that her grade school years were relatively uneventful. Her grades were slightly above average, and her attendance record was good; however, I noticed that her grade point average showed a marked decline at the beginning of eighth grade. This decline remained throughout the remainder of her junior high and high school years.

In checking her family records, number of siblings, etc., I saw that when Valerie was thirteen years old, her mother gave birth to twin boys. Two years later another baby boy arrived.

Valerie's parents came with her for her first visit. It was obvious from the onset that they were both very concerned about her. "We love Valerie, Dr. Campbell, and we are depending on you to help us figure out what our problem is."

Valerie's parents are well-dressed people who are obviously comfortable with themselves. Her father is a structural engineer, and her mother used to teach school. Their positions in the community, their involvement in their church, and their strong concern for Valerie told me that this was basically a well-developed family unit.

Why then, I wondered, *did Valerie feel so bad that suicide was her only way out?* None of her records gave any hint of a serious problem.

"What do you think, Valerie? Do you feel that you and your parents and I can answer some questions and solve some problems so that you can feel better?"

Valerie looked at me with dull, brown eyes. She held a strand of hair between her thumb and finger and constantly toyed with it. "I guess we can work something out," she answered quietly. "But I hate to see everyone going to so much trouble. I'll probably start feeling better in a day or so."

The four of us visited for the first session. Valerie's parents proudly told me of their three sons. Now and then Valerie would tell me something about one of the boys. I knew that she loved them and that she too was proud of them.

After our initial session, I asked Valerie if she would mind coming by herself next time.

"Sure, if that's OK with Mom and Dad."

At our next session, Valerie finally began to express her feelings. I soon learned that she was a 25 percenter. Until Valerie was thirteen, she was an only child. She was a good student and enjoyed school. Then the pending arrival of her twin brothers made some drastic changes in her life.

The pregnancy was a difficult one, and Valerie's mother required much bed rest. No longer could Valerie and her mother go places and do things as they had always had the freedom to do.

Unfortunately, all of this came at a time when Valerie was undergoing tremendous physical and emotional changes. Added anxieties in her life were difficult for Valerie to deal with.

"I really was glad we were going to have twins at our house, Dr. Campbell. It was exciting, but I worried a lot about Mom. I did everything she asked me to do. Dad was so used to the house being in tip-top order that he got pretty grouchy with me when I didn't keep things up the way he wanted. He was worried about Mom too, so that was probably part of the reason he was grouchy.

"So I tried not to feel bad or get mad at him when he got mad at me. Anyway, I sure was glad when the twins finally got here, and everyone was safe and healthy.

"I'll never forget the day they all came home from the hospital. I decided to surprise Mom and Dad, so I put a roast in the oven. Then I called all my friends to tell them that the twins were coming home, and I stayed on the phone for so long that the roast burned. The house smelled awful.

"When Mom and Dad and the twins came in the door, Dad was really upset, and he yelled at me. He told me that it looked like I couldn't do anything right, and he began to open doors and windows to air out the house. Then he told me to clean out the oven and fix Mother some kind of lunch while he helped her and the babies get settled. I didn't even get to hold either one of them until late that afternoon.

"From that day on, Dr. Campbell, I never felt I could do enough for Mother or Dad, and I seemed to muddle things up just trying to do them right. I felt really awful that I had ruined their homecoming, and the harder I tried to make up for it, the worse things seemed to be.

"I didn't get to spend much time with Mom after the boys got here and none at all with Dad because he took a part-time job to pay the rest of the hospital and doctor bills. Mom didn't go back to work because right after the twins' first birthday, she told me that she was pregnant again.

"Oh, I hated to hear her say that. I loved the boys, but I— actually, Dr. Campbell, sometimes I hated those boys. Everytime I needed Mom, they needed her. Everything was completely changed. I wished some of the time that they had never been born!"

Valerie dropped her head and started crying. "I feel so bad saying that," she sobbed. "Nobody in this world should hate her baby brothers, but I did."

"It wasn't wrong to have those feelings, Valerie. Did you ever tell your mother or dad how you felt?"

"No, no, Dr. Campbell. Then they really would have hated me. We had so little time together as it was. I didn't want to make them mad at me, or I wouldn't have had them at all. So I never complained or bothered them with any of my problems. But when Mother said she was going to have another baby, I wanted to die. I was so mad! I just didn't want more babies in our house. Two at once was enough. I began to hate the new baby long before it got here. And I sure couldn't talk to Mom or Dad about how I felt about the new baby. They would have been shocked."

"By the time the new baby arrived, Dad had gotten a new job, and he made a lot more money. So he hired a woman to come in and help Mother part-time. This gave me a lot of free time, and I sure didn't spend it at home. Everyone was so wrapped up in kids that they didn't even miss me. But I felt awful."

"What do you mean, Valerie. Did you feel sick?"

"No, Dr. Campbell, I mean that I felt sad all the time. I missed the times I used to have with Mom and Dad."

"Did they quit speaking to you, or did they refuse to take you places?"

"Oh, they probably would have taken me places if I had asked, but they were always working with the boys. Dad wasn't so grouchy anymore. I suppose that was because he didn't have so many money worries, but his new job kept him away from home so much that any free time he had, he spent with Mom and the boys. Once in a while they would take Sunday rides and ask me to go along, but I just didn't want to hang around those babies all the time. I bet you think I was pretty selfish, don't you?"

"Did you feel selfish, Valerie?"

"No, not selfish—just lonesome. But I made some new friends

at school, and some of them smoked pot. Anyway, they were a lot of fun, and I didn't feel as lonesome. Finally, they convinced me to try some pot, so I did. Then I really felt guilty. I knew if Mom and Dad ever found out about it, they would be awful disappointed in me."

"You are quite concerned about how other people feel about you, aren't you, Valerie?"

"Sure, shouldn't I be? I mean, after all, my parents would have died if they knew I was using pot. And my favorite neighbor and my grandpa. Oh, wow, what a disappointment I must be to all of them. But I didn't quit smoking. I felt better when I did it, but I felt guilty when I got home. The more pot I used, the worse I felt, so the more I used. Doesn't that sound stupid? Finally, nothing mattered. My parents just thought I was enjoying evenings out with my friends, and all the time I was using heavy and feeling guilty because they trusted me so much. By this time I had gone from marijuana to cocaine.

"I didn't make any waves at home because I didn't want anyone to find out what I was doing. Finally, it got to be too much. I wasn't spending any time with Mom and Dad and the boys. They didn't ask me to go places with them or to spend any time with them. I guess they thought that I was going through a phase where I was embarrassed to be with them, but if they only knew. Anyway, I just drifted away from them. Nothing mattered to me but cocaine. One night a bunch of us got together and got to acting stupid, and I took a bunch of pills, and here I am.

"I told all my friends that I was going to take the pills because I wanted to die. But the craziest thing, Dr. Campbell, I didn't really think I'd die. I was kind of thinking that maybe my parents would see how bad I felt and love me again. So maybe you are dealing with a 'crazy' here. Who else but a crazy person would announce that she wanted to die and take some pills and then hope she wouldn't die?"

Valerie's parents were shocked when they finally, through sessions of painful counseling, became aware of how she felt.

"O Valerie, if only you had said something," her father said through choked back tears. "Oh, how insensitive I was to your needs."

"I want to stress something to both of you," I interrupted. "As parents you were doing all you knew how to do at the time. Neither of you were aware of the 25 percenter personality trait of your daughter. Neither of you had ever encountered adolescent depression. Many times it is difficult even for professionals to detect. Don't let the guilt get in the way of the healing process."

After some weeks of both family and individual counseling, even sometimes including Valerie's three little brothers, Valerie's self-esteem began to improve, and her depression lifted. She became aware of her strengths and weaknesses and learned that she was not responsible for all the problems of the world. And her parents learned how to be more responsive to her needs, drawing her into their conversations when they felt she should be expressing her feelings. It wasn't easy for them to try to pull Valerie's worries into the open because they had always been used to a quiet, relatively problem-free Valerie.

They are bright, sensitive parents, however, and not only will Valerie benefit from the pain she had to suffer, but her brothers will also. I'm sure that Valerie's parents will apply their new-found skills in rearing the boys.

Happily, I couldn't help but notice the gradual change in Valerie's physical appearance as she counseled with us. The last session I had with her, I noticed that she had changed her hairstyle and was neatly and stylishly dressed. Helping people like Valerie and her family is what makes my work so rewarding.

Identifying Teenage Depression
Valerie's case reveals how important it is to find ways to identify teenage depression. I want to stress to you that depression *can* be cured. If you feel that you child is suffering from depression, be sure to contact anyone with whom he comes in contact on a daily basis, such as, teachers, school counselor, and youth workers. Ask them to help you look for the warning signals of teenage depression, listed on the following pages:

● If your child is only mildly depressed, you will notice that he is not able to keep his mind focused on a subject as long as he once could. He is experiencing *short attention span*. His mind will drift, and he will become easily distracted. The most obvious example of this shortened attention span will be seen when your teen tries to do his homework. He will find it difficult to concentrate on his work, and the harder he tries, the less he will get done. This will result in frustration and feelings of inadequacy. He will blame himself, thinking he is just plain dumb. His self-esteem will suffer because he sees this inability to do his homework as a lack of intellectual ability.

● *Daydreaming* is another very common manifestation of depression. This will be noticed in the classroom. As the depression increases, your child's ability to concentrate and be attentive in class will decrease. At this point the teacher is the best person to identify the problem. Quite naturally, however, many teachers see daydreaming as laziness or poor attitude. And often that is just the case. At this point I must mention that one or two symptoms of depression do not warrant a diagnosis of true depression. We usually see a gradual development of a whole constellation of symptoms.

● The result of short attention span and daydreaming will almost always be a *drop in grades*. This drop is so subtle that it often goes unnoticed for a period of time. Most parents and teachers see this gradual drop simply as a lack of interest in a subject. Because the grades slowly go from an A to an A- to a B and so on, depression is seldom seen as the culprit in the grade drop.

● *Boredom* is normal in teens, especially early adolescents, but only for short periods of time. For example, your teen may hang around the house for an hour or two or maybe two whole days, acting bored. She may even state that she is bored. Don't become alarmed and diagnose her as depressed. But if her boredom is prolonged, lasting several days, this could very well be an early warning signal that something is wrong. You will notice that she wants to stay by herself in her own room for long periods of time. She will just lie on her bed and daydream or listen to music. Everything that normally interested her will no longer pull her out of this mood. Few things worry me as much as prolonged boredom in an adolescent, especially an early adolescent.

● At this stage of depression, your teen begins to suffer from *somatic depression.* Even though all depression is physiological, or has a biochemical-neurohormonal basis, at this point the symptoms begin to affect your teen in a directly physical way. She has now slipped into moderate depression. She begins to experience headaches or lower midchest pains. She may make vague complaints of stomachaches.

● Finally, your teen is feeling so miserable that she will begin to *withdraw from friends.* She will not just simply stay away from them. She will become belligerent and hostile toward them so that the ensuing unpleasantness will result in total alienation. Now, this is the point where drugs can enter the picture. Your teen will become very lonely and could very well start associating with unwholesome peers. This is where peer pressure or peer influence comes in and can be the cause of initial drug experimentation. But as you can see, peers would not be the only cause of drug involvement. Depression would also be a cause.

The most amazing fact about your teen's depression at this point is that she does not recognize it. She is miserable, and her mental and physical pain at this stage are at times unbearable. It is at this level of depression that she will begin to "act out" her feelings of misery and distress.

Doing something which has an air of excitement about it seems to somewhat relieve the pain of depression. One of the most common behaviors seen in depressed boys is breaking and entering. Boys also steal, lie, fight, drive fast, or exhibit any number of antisocial behavioral attitudes.

One of my first concerns for a teen who is referred to me for breaking and entering is to find how much depression has played into his behavior. (We must note that breaking and entering is done for more reasons than depression.) Here again, we see the need for the treatment of the whole child. Sadly, many who deal with teens focus only on the behavior, not on the underlying problem.

Because of unhealthy, violence-oriented models in the media, girls are beginning to act out their depression violently too, although not as often as boys. The pain of depression felt by girls tends to be alleviated during the close physical relationship of intercourse, and so promiscuity is common for a depressed girl. When the act is over, however, the unfortunate girl feels guilty and becomes even more depressed.

Depression can cause a child to fail at school or attempt suicide. It almost always prompts drug use and abuse. Drugs block the pain of depression. Unfortunately, when the drug is out of the teen's system, he feels worse, so he needs more. This is the way he becomes addicted to drugs. You can readily see that peer pressure does not stand alone as the cause of drug abuse. Depression is also a major cause of drug use.

Adolescent depression is complex because of its many complicated causes and effects. It is subtle because it almost always goes undetected, and it is extremely dangerous because, left undetected, suicide can result. And adolescent depression can so very easily go undetected.

Teen depression is not as easy to identify as adult depression. An adult actually *looks* depressed while a teen in mild depression acts normally, showing no outward signs of depression. It is a problem that even a parent has trouble detecting.

When a teen is moderately depressed, though, the content of his speech is often affected. He dwells primarily on depressing subjects, such as, death, morbid problems, and crises. Since many adults today seem to dwell on pessimistic trains of thought, a teen's depression may again go unnoticed.

If you see any signs of moderate depression in your child, keep a close (not smothering) eye on him. The earlier depression is identified, the less likely it is to develop into other problems. But even severe depression in teens can go undetected, so don't get down on yourself if you do not detect your teen's depression, no matter what state it is in.

Teens mask their depression when they are with other people

and let down when they are alone. Knowing this can be a great help to parents. If you suspect that your child is depressed, try to view her sometime when she is not aware of your presence. Then you will be able to see how miserable she really is. This is not the best way to identify depression, but at least it is a start toward helping your child.

It is crucial to understand the total constellation of symptoms of depression in detail because one or two symptoms may or may not signify true depression. True depression is a biochemical and neurohormonal process that usually develops slowly over a period of weeks or months. A severely depressed teen may, at times, exhibit some of the classic symptoms of adult depression, such as, feelings of helplessness, hopelessness, despondency, and despair. The teen may also experience sleeping problems, eating problems (eating too much or too little), lack of energy, and difficulty in handling anger.

Curing and Preventing Depression

Depression can be cured, so don't become overly anxious about your child's depression. Early identification can halt the insidious progress of depression.

To initially prevent depression from happening to your child, it is crucial, first of all to show him that you love him and care about him. You can do this by spending enough time with him that his psychological defenses can come down, and then he will be able to meaningfully communicate with you. Then your love-giving, that is, eye contact, physical contact, and focused attention, will be meaningful to him.

Adolescent depression is not something you can consider a phase that will pass. This affliction tends to grow worse and worse unless it is identified and intervention steps are taken. Given appropriate help, however, early teens are quite able to overcome depression.

The best way to describe it is absolute terror. I would count the kids and the paragraphs. With each one reading one paragraph aloud, I could figure out when my turn was coming, and I dreaded it because they always laughed when I tried to read. One day, when I was in the fourth grade, I wet my pants.

Mary, age 18, alcoholic

Drugs and the "Special" Child

Every child is special. But the term *special child* is specifically used to refer to a child with what we call learning disabilities. Your child may or may not fall into this group, but you need to know some basics about these disabilities and how they relate to drug use.

Let's start with another true-false quiz. The answers will become obvious to you as you proceed through the chapter.

True   False

1. Most children outgrow learning disabilities.
2. Children with learning disabilities are predominantly male.
3. Most people with learning disabilities have slightly below-average IQs.

4. Early detection is extremely important in helping your child cope with learning disabilities.
5. Specific clues are usually obvious in a learning disabled child.
6. Hyperactivity is quite common in learning disabled children.
7. Hyperactive children use drugs to ease their anger and frustration.
8. Learning disabled children are totally unaware of their problem.
9. The low self-esteem felt by most learning disabled kids is a prime cause of drug use.

Before going any further, I would like for you to try an experiment. Find a simple maze. (You should be able to find one in a child's coloring book or activity book.) Now, place the maze flat on a desk or table and prop a mirror directly behind it. Sitting at the desk or table, take a pencil in hand and trace the path through the maze looking only in the mirror. Don't cheat. Look only in the mirror as you guide the pencil through the maze.

How did you get along? That was a frustrating experience, wasn't it?

As you look at the irregular lines you drew in your attempt to get through the maze, try to imagine a teacher saying, "That's very nice," or "My, you're doing much better than you did yesterday."

You are an intelligent person. You know that you did not do good work. And if you were a learning disabled student, you would be an intelligent person, and you could tell by comparing your work with the work of your fellow students that you did not do as well as they did. Imagine the embarrassment and frustration. That experiment gives you a vague idea of the embarrassment and frustrations the learning disabled child faces every day.

The Trials of Having a Learning Disability

Studies, especially educational studies, show that 5 to 15 percent of our nation's school-age population is learning disabled (Madeline Lee, "Parenting: Why Josh Isn't Dumb," *Ms Magazine*, June 1987, p. 66). But about 25 to 60 percent of the patients we see in our clinic are learning disabled.

The Federal Government states: "Children with specific learning disabilities exhibit a disorder in one or more of the basic psychological processes involved in understanding spoken or written language. These may be manifested in disorders of listening, thinking, talking, reading, writing, spelling, or arithmetic" (Public Law 94-142).

Unfortunately, emotional disturbances and behavioral difficulties are also usually prevalant in a learning disabled child. All too often, these children are labeled as "stubborn behavior problems who could learn if they wanted to." This label dooms the child to failure and more often than not, he drops out of school. Today, authorities agree that these are usually bright children, and when their problem is diagnosed early, they can be given assistance in their weak areas and go on to complete an education.

ACLD, the Association for Children with Learning Disabilities, conducted a study of the correlation between children with learning disabilities and juvenile delinquents. The study was drawn from three metropolitan areas and included approximately 1,000 adjudicated delinquents and 1,000 youths with no record of adjudication. Thirty-two percent of the delinquent boys were found to be learning disabled (*Prevalence of Handicapped Juveniles in the Justice System: A Survey of the Literature*, p. 48).

Sadly, studies also tell us that learning disabled children suffer from low self-esteem. The mental abuse these children suffer leaves lifetime scars. And the pain of suffering a learning disability does not stop with the sufferer himself; statistics show that parents of learning disabled children show a high rate of divorce (*The Hidden Handicap*, ACLD Foundation, p. 5).

Due to the fact that learning disabilities almost invariably lead to problems of depression, anger, anxiety, passive-aggressive behavior, and low self-esteem, the incidence of drug abuse in these children is extremely high. Imagine the frustration and anger felt by these kids.

Johnny Alton has a learning disability. He has dyslexia. This means that Johnny has difficulty perceiving the written word. Letters sometimes appear in reverse to him or do not appear at all. He also has difficulty writing and spelling. Unfortunately, this diagnosis of dyslexia was not made until Johnny became a frustrated, angry teen and turned to drugs.

I'll not forget the day I got the results of Johnny's tests, and I could tell him why he was having trouble reading and spelling. "Johnny," I began, "we have finally completed your tests, and now I am ready to give you some answers. I have seen, in reviewing your school records, that you have had a great deal of trouble since the third grade."

"That's right, Dr. Campbell," he agreed. "I just couldn't keep up with my teachers. I didn't know what they were talkin' about half the time. I usually just sat and stared out the window, but then I would get into trouble for that. I've gotten into a lot of trouble since I started to school. I guess I'm just a big dummy."

"No, Johnny, you're not dumb. You have a reading difficulty which is called 'dyslexia.' The fact that you have such trouble reading is not your fault. You were probably born with the inability to read well. But you are a good listener, and you are not dumb."

Johnny looked relieved. "You mean there's something wrong that keeps me from reading? You mean I'm just a normal person? I have this dyslexia thing, but I am just a normal person?"

"Yes, Johnny. And we are going to work with your school and try to get you some help so that learning can be as interesting for you as it is for some of your friends."

"I don't know if school could ever be fun, Dr. Campbell, but it might be different now." Johnny became serious. "But, Dr. Campbell, someone my age should be able to read. What are people gonna say? Do other people have this? Is it curable? You know, I've always tried to hide the fact that I can't read 'cause I've been ashamed of it. Are they gonna find out now?"

Johnny has some uphill battles to face, but at least we know his problem. We have a starting point.

Diagnosing the problem does not cure it. Johnny will go through a time of bitterness and resentment for having a reading problem. But we will encourage him to face his problem. These feelings are very normal, but with counseling, Johnny should be able to put the past behind him and go on with his education.

Perceptual Problems

A learning disability is also a perceptual problem. Nobody has perfect perception. Everybody perceives in a different way; it is a matter of degree. The degree of Johnny's reading problem is severe, but he is not retarded. He is a bright young man who is very capable of learning. He has a normal IQ.

When we hear of someone having difficulty reading, we automatically think of the written word. We don't stop to think that reading numbers and, yes, even facial expressions is also a problem. Social situations can be extremely frustrating for the learning or perceptually disabled individual.

One of my patients, a learning disabled high school senior explained it this way: "I had to spend so much time studying that I had little time for a social life. But I didn't really mind because I found being in crowds very difficult. I was forever thinking someone was mad at me, when actually they were just tired or upset about something totally unrelated to me."

These kids have a difficult time making friends. They see all the other kids talking and spending time together, but they just can't seem to fit in. The learning disabled child feels that everyone else knows exactly what to say and how to act. Finally, he considers himself a dismal failure and stops trying.

Recently I talked to a young girl who went completely through school without a proper diagnosis of her learning problem. "My early education was dreadful," she recalled. "I was always saying the wrong things or falling all over somebody. Everybody teased me and called me a 'klutz.' My teachers would say, 'Oh, don't worry. She's a girl. Schooling doesn't matter for her. She'll end up married.'

"They ended up putting me in a 'special class' which was really a class for retarded students, and all the other kids called us 'retards.' I came out of the whole thing with a poor self-image, but now that I know what has been wrong with me all these years, I think I am going to make it. I'm studying to be a counselor. I think I can make a real contribution helping other learning disabled people."

The pain suffered by all these wonderful people can be, and often is, a reason to become involved in drugs. Drugs block pain, feelings of low self-esteem, and the depression and anger caused by years of frustration and suffering.

The Added Problem of Hyperactivity

Learning disabled people almost always have a "piggyback" problem called hyperactivity. Authorities are in general agreement that these problems are present at birth. In rare cases they can be caused by encephalitis or trauma, but the vast majority are present at birth.

What a world these children live in. Not only do they have trouble with perception, but they are also hyperactive. This does not always mean that they are overactive. One major aspect of hyperactivity is a short attention span. The hyperactive child cannot keep his mind on a task long enough to really learn or absorb what he should. Because his attention span is short, he jumps from one thing to another faster than other children normally would.

I am reminded of a story about Rick, a learning disabled and hyperactive boy who was playing a video game with a friend. Rick's mother said, "Dr. Campbell, for the first time Rick was about to win the game, but I could see that his excitement was going to be his downfall. He is aware of his problems and has devised ways to cope with them. On this particular day, he called to me with great excitement, 'Mom, Mom, come in here quick; you gotta hold me down! I'm afraid I'm gonna jump outta this chair before I beat him.'

"And so I did," the mother went on. "I went into the family room and placed my hands on his shoulders. 'You can do it,

Rick, you can do it,' I whispered, and sure enough, he did.

Hyperactive children have great difficulty in the academic world. Their minds are constantly jumping. Their ability to think rationally, logically, or sequentially is minimal. Behavior control is a task of Herculean proportions for them.

They quickly switch from one thing to another which makes them appear to be overactive and fast. Even if they want to spend time on one task, such as playing a video game with a friend, they can't because they just have to jump from one thing to another.

All of this activity causes problems for them at school. They really can't sit still. They can't keep from talking and pestering their classmates. They are quickly labeled as the class behavior problem or the "class clown." Left undetected until adolescence, these problems compound, and the child is a prime candidate for using drugs simply because by this point he is so confused and angry.

Look at Johnny Alton. His particular learning disability was not diagnosed until he had come to our clinic. All his life, Johnny thought he was dumb. He had terrible self-esteem. He became very depressed.

And that's how the majority of these kids feel. They give up and assume they are dumb. They feel unloved and unlovable. They cannot focus long enough to understand other people's feelings, so they think nobody loves or cares about them; therefore, they rarely develop close friendships.

By the time they reach adolescence, they are so filled with anger that depression becomes a major problem. Now they have two sources of depression: feelings of being unlovable and worthless, and anger at not being loved. This double dose of depression is a perfect reason to take drugs. These kids are hurting, and they know from experimentation that drugs can take the hurt away.

School and the Learning Disabled Child

At this point, let me give you a broad survey of the academic years of a learning disabled child from elementary school through either high school graduation or possibly dropping out of school.

From the beginning, school is one negative experience after another. Usually after the first and second grades things begin to get difficult. During the latter part of the third grade or the beginning of the fourth grade, most teachers, almost without realizing it, take their class from concrete learning to learning by abstract concepts. It is practically impossible for these kids to make that change. They are not mature enough to do it. They can do a lot of memorizing during the first two or three grades, but when abstract thinking is presented, these kids can't cope. Understanding goes out the window. Most of them recognize this frustrating change without understanding the cause for it.

For instance, Johnny Alton told me that he really liked school when he first started, but by the time he got into the third or fourth grade, everything started going wrong for him. He kept trying, but to no avail. He vividly and painfully remembers trying to memorize everything the teacher said so that he could pretend he was reading and that he understood what was going on. Finally, it didn't work anymore. He gave up and became the "class clown" to cover up his misery. He struggled along in this manner through his sophomore year in high school. By this time, drugs had become well entrenched in his life. They relieved his pain.

Most of these kids, including Johnny, usually exert one final act of determination toward academics. This usually occurs in the fourth grade. They do pretty well with this burst of total sacrifice because they want to learn and be like the rest of the kids in their class. But they can't keep up the pace indefinitely. They finally fall apart, and depression sets in. It is during the early stages of their depression that tics start developing. Tics are sudden movements of parts of the body; for example, heavy blinking, head jerking, sudden grimacing.

Children can disguise these tics beautifully. One of the classic examples of a tic is head jerks, especially in boys. (Learning disabilities are most common in male children; some females have them, but they are much more predominant in the male population.) Boys purposely let their hair grow long so that when their heads jerk, they give the appearance of tossing their hair out of their eyes.

Kids use many other ways to disguise tics, but you can walk into any classroom, look carefully, and see kids "ticing" all over the place. Tics are almost always caused by academic pressure. It is just heartbreaking to see kids "ticing" because the child is obviously going through a kind of torture. Of course, tics don't do any good. The child doesn't get any positive feedback from his particular tic. He only gets more and more frustrated and depressed.

Now here is where the picture really gets complicated because, as I stated earlier, childhood depression is very difficult to detect. Since a short attention span is a sign of childhood depression as well as a sign of hyperactivity, many professionals overlook it as a sign of depression. They assume a short attention span means a child is hyperactive, so they prescribe Ritalin, a medication which affects a child's brain and brings his attention span to normal.

When a child's short attention span is really caused by depression, Ritalin is not effective. Ritalin cannot help cure the emotional problems of a depressed child. When a depressed child's attention span does not improve, most professionals assume the problem is due to hyperactivity, so more Ritalin is prescribed. Of course, this doesn't do any good because depression is the culprit, but the Ritalin dosage is increased periodically. The child gets worse and worse.

And these are the kids who get into drugs very early in their lives. Improper diagnosis causes pain and frustration, and drugs ease pain and frustration. These kids don't quite understand why they feel the way they do, but they know for sure that drugs take the pain away. It is worthwhile to point out again that treatment of the whole child is imperative. When a learning disabled child is involved with drugs, a whole battery of problems is the cause for this involvement.

Few people realize that learning disabilities and hyperactivity are physical problems. They are, however, just as physical a problem as a broken arm, and they must be dealt with.

No one should treat just the drug abuse of these kids without understanding and treating all the underlying reasons. Drug use is just the tip of the iceberg. Just curing the physical addiction will be a waste of time because the child will almost always go right back to taking drugs as soon as he has the opportunity.

Johnny Alton told me that even though he hated school, his homework at least gave him some time with his mother. "She would sit by the hour, Dr. Campbell, and work on my reading with me. I hated it so bad I wanted to throw up, but I kept tryin' 'cause she would stay right there beside me.

"One time when I was in grade school, I was supposed to memorize a poem. My mom helped me pick one out. I think it was one she liked real well. Anyway, I can still remember some of that poem. It was called, 'A Bird Came Down the Walk.' It goes something like this: 'A bird came down the walk, it did not know I saw. It bit an angleworm in halves and ate the fellow raw. I don't know how the rest of it goes, but that much sticks with me. You probably think I'm silly, but that poem, or part of it anyway, has stayed with me for quite a while. Everytime I think of it, I can see Mom and me sittin' at the kitchen table and her tryin' to teach it to me."

"I don't think you're silly, Johnny. Remembering that poem proves to me what I already knew—you are a bright young man."

"Yeah, sure. But I'll tell you who is smart and that is my old man. When he's not drinkin', he's not bad. He knows lots of interesting things. I sure wish he would come in and talk to you. Mom keeps askin' him to, but he won't. He just gets mad. Oh, well, there's no sense thinkin' about it. He won't and that's that."

I didn't tell Johnny, but his mother said that there is a chance that his "old man" will come to a counseling session. She said that he is pleased to see the progress Johnny is making. Maybe he will come. But as Johnny says, I won't count on it. I hope he does because total family involvement in the drug problem of any of its members is crucial to the treatment of the person.

Identifying a Learning Disabled Child

In addition to observing your child's academic progress, several other clues can help you determine if your child should be tested for perceptual handicaps. I urge you to seek help as soon as possible. The earlier he is tested and the earlier the educational intervention begins, the easier time he will have during his school years.

The Association for Children with Learning Disabilities (ACLD) offers the following list of common clues identifying learning disabled preschoolers:

1. Does your preschooler love "Sesame Street"?
   Most preschoolers with learning disabilities don't.
2. Does your preschooler love to listen to records?
   Some preschoolers with learning disabilities don't.
3. Does your preschooler love to look at picture books?
   Some preschoolers with learning disabilities don't.
4. Does your preschooler enjoy playing with children his own age?
   Most preschoolers with learning disabilities don't.
5. Does your preschooler seem to march "to a different drummer?"
   Most preschoolers with learning disabilities do.

Listed below are some common statements from parents of learning disabled children, compiled by ACLD. Again, if you see your child in more than one of these statements, testing might be in order.

- *He knocks into the building blocks, bumps into the door, falls out of his chair, crashes into his playmates, and catapults himself through space.*
- *She can talk about topiary trees, but she can't zip her zipper or draw a circle and hates putting toys and puzzles together.*
- *He looks at everything, but doesn't seem to see—in fact, his hands seem to see better than his eyes.*
- *Her big eyes look up at me, and she listens, but I don't seem to be getting through to her.*

- *He understands everything I say to him, but he doesn't express himself well, not at all like his brothers and sisters.*
- *He overreacts or underreacts to everything—it's like his internal thermostat is not working.*
- *She's nine years old, but acts much younger.*
- *He never seems put together right, and yet I dress him better than many of his friends and fuss over him a lot.*
- *She's so smart, yet she has the attention span of a flea—she jiggles all day long, flits from one thing to another, and sometimes sounds like a broken record.*
- *He never lets me hug him. As a matter of fact, it seems any display of affection makes him uncomfortable.*

You can see the utter frustration both the parent and the learning disabled child go through on a daily basis.

If you have found your child in any of these statements, you *may* have a learning disabled child; however, sometimes a learning disabled child exhibits none of these symptoms.

Help for the Learning Disabled Child

If you do find that your child is learning disabled, don't despair. The younger he is when the diagnosis is made, the greater his chances for intervention to make his life much easier. By the same token, the longer the problem goes undiagnosed, the greater the chances for drug use.

Before I end this chapter, I have some good news to tell you. Early one morning, just as I stepped into my office, my secretary handed me a telephone number to call. "This person is quite anxious to talk with you, Dr. Campbell," she said. "He has called five or six times just this morning. He wouldn't leave his name, only this number."

I didn't recognize the number, but I immediately returned the call. "This is Dr. Campbell," I began. "I am returning your call."

"Yeah, Doc. This is Johnny Alton's father. I think I should talk to you."

I was surprised and pleased that Mr. Alton finally made the decision to talk. "Sure, Mr. Alton. Let me check my schedule with my secretary, and I'll set up an appointment with you."

"I don't wanna wait, Doc. The sooner the better before I back out on this. I'm at work. I'll call you back in fifteen minutes. That should give you enough time to figure somethin' out. I haven't told Johnny or his mother about this yet, so I'll appreciate it if you don't. That's why I'm callin' from work."

I was anxious to meet Johnny's father. Johnny was making some progress, and his mother was already attending some sessions. I set up an appointment for the end of the day.

When the scheduled time arrived, I found a nervous father pacing the floor in my office, smoking one cigarette after another. When I walked in, I offered him a chair, but he declined saying, "I talk better standing up. You see, Doc, I've started going to A.A. meetings, you know, Alcoholics Anonymous. I haven't told Johnny and his mother yet, but I will.

"See, since my drinkin' didn't keep me from work, I didn't ever see that there was any problem with it. Oh, I've missed a day or two now and then, but nothing to cause me to lose my job. Anyway, I'm here because of Johnny. I need to tell you somethin'. I don't even know if my wife really knows this, but I can't read any better than Johnny. And when his mother came home and told me about what he has—that dyslexic, or whatever it is—it dawned on me that that's probably what I've got.

"I always figured I was just dumb. It's always been hard to find a job not bein' able to read an' all, but I've never let my family starve. I can read some, now and then, but it's not easy. I don't read books or anything like that and I don't read the newspaper either, but I sure do listen close.

"I never have told anyone about this before, Doc, 'cause I figured they'd just tell me I was dumb and I didn't need that. I quit school when I was sixteen 'cause I was always in trouble and I didn't make any good grades—just like Johnny. But I found a job doin' construction work and I've been doin' it ever since. But you're the first person I've ever told. I suppose my teachers knew about it or maybe they didn't. Maybe they just thought I was ornery and dumb. I sure caused them enough trouble to think that. I spent most of my school time in some detention room or in the principal's office.

"But when Johnny got into all this trouble and you found out that he couldn't read and you even said that he's not dumb and mean, just has this dyslexic thing—well, I got to thinkin'. Is it somethin' he got from me?"

"Many professionals are saying that dyslexia is hereditary," I answered him. "We still have a lot to be learned about these kinds of problems, but what we do know is that when people are dyslexic, their lives can become pretty difficult at times."

"At times? You mean all the time. There's not a day goes by that I don't have to figure out how to get around not bein' able to read. For instance, whenever Johnny's mother asks me to pick up some stuff at the grocery store, I have an awful time figurin' it out. What I don't get, I just tell her I forgot. Sometimes she makes me a list, but that don't help much. We usually have some kind of a fight about a simple thing like pickin' up a few groceries.

"I get real nervous when the boss gives me a supply list to pick up. Usually I just tell the people workin' at the place where I pick up the stuff that I left my glasses in the truck and they read the list and get the stuff for me. It's a hard way to go, Doc, real hard.

"And so when I found out that Johnny has the same kind of problem, I figured I should say something. He's a good boy in his own way, Doc. He doesn't mean nobody any harm. But he sure has been in trouble lately. I think I know how he feels. See, it just gets the best of you, and my way out is to get good and drunk. I guess his way out is to get stoned on drugs. The trouble with that is that you can get hooked on the stuff.

"I'll be the one to tell Johnny and his mother that I came in here and I'll tell them that I'm going to A.A. meetings. I don't know what will come of all this. Maybe somethin' good will. Guess we'll just have to wait and see. I don't know what Johnny's mother will think when I tell her all of this. They'll be comin' in in a day or two. Maybe I'll come with them. I don't know yet. Everything is comin' too fast, but I'll try, I'll try."

With that, Johnny's father left my office. I hope he makes up his mind, not only to come with Johnny and his mother, but also to seek professional help for his alcoholism and continue with A.A. Johnny said he didn't drink alcohol, but he did, and he learned to be an alcoholic from his father. Alcoholism, drug addiction, and even learning disabilities are family problems. Neither Johnny nor his father can simply "get over" the problem on an individual basis. The entire Alton family needs to work together on this. The problem is not just Johnny's addiction. It is not just Mr. Alton's addiction. It is a family problem.

Now that you have some insight into the world of the learning disabled, it might be helpful for you to go back to the true and false quiz at the beginning of this chapter and see if any of your answers have changed. As I said to Johnny's father, we still have much to learn about learning disabilities, but what we do know is that these children and adults are not retarded. They can learn. As a friend once said to me, "These kids have to go someplace else to get there; they can't get there from here." In other words, they can learn; it's just that we have to teach them in a different way. The disability itself is not curable, but the learning disabled person *can* learn and develop coping skills.

As I have already stated, early detection is of the utmost importance. (The list of symptoms given earlier in this chapter will help you to determine whether or not your child should be tested.) Early detection will enable a child to learn to cope with his particular disability at an early age instead of having to wonder why he can't do things like other kids. Learning disabled kids realize, at a young age, that they have some kind of problem. They just don't understand what it is. They constantly compare themselves to their peers. And, of course, when they see that they aren't measuring up to the expectations of their teachers, parents, and friends, they lose self-esteem. Then drugs often enter the picture.

Drugs and Children with Severe Mental/Neurological Problems

In this chapter I'm going to deal with some neurological problems that cause drug use and abuse. Neurological problems are quite often overlooked in diagnosing the cause of drug abuse simply because the use of drugs masks the problem. I will not go into a detailed description of all neurological problems (that would take another book), but I do want to make you aware of the fact that they too are a major cause of drug abuse.

A neurological problem is an actual physical brain dysfunction. In this chapter I am going to discuss only two neurological problems which cause severe mental problems: bipolar affective disorder and borderline personality disorder. Before I discuss these disorders, consider the statements on the next page. Don't worry if some of these terms seem confusing; the meaning of each term will become clear to you in the discussion that follows.

89

1. Bipolar affective is a neurological disorder. It has an organic basis.
2. Bipolar affective disorder is not curable, but it can be treated and brought under control.
3. Lithium carbonate is an effective drug in the treatment of bipolar affective disorder.
4. Borderline personality disorder resembles both a neurological disorder and a personality disorder.
5. Drugs and alcohol alleviate the pain suffered by people with borderline personality disorder.
6. People with borderline personality disorder have such a strong sense of worthlessness that they achieve little self-identity and, therefore, have difficulty becoming individuals in their own right.

We find that about 60 percent of today's kids are just experimenting with drugs while 40 percent have gone on to abuse and addiction (*Drug Scene Update*, PRIDE, 1987). I am finding that about 10 percent of those who abuse drugs and are addicted to them have serious mental/neurological problems and are self-medicating. In other words, they use drugs and alcohol just to get through the day. To ask these kids to "just say no" to drugs is an impossibility because without their drugs, they cannot function adequately and become quite confused in their thinking. They could even become psychotic. Unfortunately, the drugs they use mask the real problem. So you can readily see the dilemma faced by these kids.

Generally, mental/neurological problems can be treated with the proper prescription drug once a proper diagnosis is made. Kids with these problems are the kids who are most harmed by a single diagnosis program. For instance, one of these kids may be a troublemaker in his school and also be caught using drugs. He is sent to a psychologist who talks to him about his temper and encourages him to quit using drugs. He may be sent to a residential or an outpatient program which fails to do an adequate evaluation, and the underlying illness goes undiagnosed. In this all-too-common situation, the teenager is counseled for his drug problem, but the primary problem, his mental/neurological disorder, goes untreated.

You can bet that just as soon as this kid is back on the streets, he'll be back on drugs. He has to take drugs. He cannot function without them. His mental/neurological disorder is the cause for the drug abuse, and only a complete evaluation of the child will uncover this reason for drug use and open the door for effective treatment.

Bipolar Affective Disorder

Now let's consider the two severe mental/neurological disorders I mentioned earlier in this chapter. Both disorders can result in drug and alcohol abuse. First, let's deal with bipolar affective disorder. (It may be more familiar to you as manic-depressive psychosis.) It can be a devastating illness if improperly diagnosed and left untreated.

Bipolar affective disorder causes mood swings from elation to depression. The cycles are not particularly related to any external excessive excitement. Kids suffering from bipolar affective disorder often show poor judgment by carrying jokes too far, destroying property, or becoming argumentative when they are in the manic phase. In general, they show excessive excitement.

They may speak rapidly and talk of unrealistically grand ideas, and they jump rapidly from topic to topic. Their friends begin to avoid them, finding them abrasive.

During the depressive phase, the sufferer finds himself sleeping more than usual and feeling very lethargic. But when the major phase of depression sets in, he becomes agitated and suffers insomnia. He withdraws socially and becomes extremely irritable. Some attempt suicide "on the way down," reporting that they fear experiencing the full depths of depression again.

Amy, a patient at our clinic, has a bipolar affective disorder. Her use of drugs and alcohol had helped her to maintain a kind of emotional stability, but an improper diagnosis had resulted in the removal of drugs, and she became very depressed. I am *not* saying that these kids *should* be given illicit drugs on a daily basis. I *am* saying that they need a thorough evaluation and a diagnosis which would allow them to receive proper treatment and prescription medication if necessary.

In our first visit together Amy just dropped her head, allowing her long, brown hair to fall in her face and stared at the floor.

"Is there anything you'd like to talk about, Amy?" I began.

"Not really. I just want to get out of here."

"Things aren't going so well for you at home, I understand." I began again. "Would you like to tell me something about that?"

"I think my mother and I hate each other. We don't get along at all."

"Why do you suppose you don't get along?"

"I just get fed up with her bossing me all the time. I don't always feel like doing everything she wants me to do. And when she wants me to do anything, she wants it right now. I can never say, 'Wait a minute' or 'Let me finish this, first.' If I do, she starts harping."

"Is that why you attempted suicide? You just wanted to get away from your mother?" Gradually, my questions prompted Amy to tell her story.

"No. See, it's like this, Dr. Campbell. My mom and I had this big fight. And everything else in my life was awful. I felt down all the time, and I wasn't getting along with my friends. Nothing mattered. So, the night I took the pills, I just went into the bathroom because I knew Mom was in there, and I threw all my empty pill bottles in the sink. I just wanted Mom to hurt as bad as I was hurting, and I wanted to die.

"It seems like ever since I've been in junior high nothing has gone right for me. Mom and I fight, and I get these feelings of being really down in the dumps. Anyway, one day when I was in junior high, a kid offered me some marijuana, so I tried it. At first it was not a big deal, but then I began to like it. It made me feel good.

"From there I did some other stuff, and then Mom and Dad found out about it and took me to a counselor. We all talked to him for a few weeks, and he decided that Mom and I needed to communicate better and all would be well at our house.

"So we tried for a while, but I started back on marijuana again. I didn't see any harm in it. Anyway, I was communicating with Mom, so she thought I was doing just great.

"But one day I got that awful down feeling again, and the stuff I was using wasn't doing me too much good, so I went a little heavy on it. That was when Mom and Dad found out about me using drugs again and drinking, and they hauled me off to some psycho ward. I didn't stay there very long, though. They said basically the same thing, that Mom and I were going to have to learn how to tolerate each other and open some lines of communication. So we tried again. And that's how it's been going. One shrink after another. One thing for sure—Mom and I sure do communicate now, but I can't stand her, and I don't think she can stand me. She told me the other day that I would have to take some responsibility for this problem or get out.

"I didn't have any place to go, and I got to feeling awful so I guess I just decided that I would be better off dead. The night that I did it, I walked through the family room and saw Mom and Dad laughing and talking and having a good time watching TV, and for some reason, I couldn't handle that. It made me furious to see them so happy when I felt so hideous. I guess I blew a fuse. I don't know. I do know that I decided right then and there that I didn't want to live, so I took some of anything I could find.

"But since I did it, I don't feel so proud of myself. In fact, I feel really stupid. Do you think I am crazy, Dr. Campbell?"

I assured Amy that she was not crazy. I told her that after we did a thorough evaluation of her, we would have some answers.

Our evaluation helped us determine that, among other things, Amy does have a bipolar affective disorder. A lengthy talk with her parents uncovered some interesting information that she has two paternal aunts who also have symptoms of bipolar affective disorder. Research is finding that bipolar affective disorder can indeed be inherited. This means that it can have an organic basis. *Organic* here means neurological—a problem with tissue damage or dysfunction. At any rate, it is treatable. Amy's case will take time because her illness went undiagnosed for a great length of time, causing many areas of her life to be affected.

Her family is involved in her treatment which is a tremendously positive step, so with a lot of work and patience, I feel we can help her get her life back in order without relying on illicit drugs and alcohol.

Larry's Story

Remember Larry Schmidt, the boy I mentioned at the beginning of this book? Larry is the boy who is working in the bakery so he can buy better weed. Larry also has a bipolar affective disorder. Even though we diagnosed Larry's problem earlier than Amy's, he will go through some rough times because his parents are not consistent with his treatment. They are having difficulty accepting the fact that their son has a condition requiring prescription medications as part of the treatment.

I admitted Larry to the hospital because he too had attempted suicide. He continues to be quite suicidal and needs some inpatient care. He is an angry boy. His road to recovery won't be easy mainly because he fights against it and his parents are not as involved in his treatment as they should be. (I hate to admit adolescents to the hospital, and I try to avoid it as much as possible; however, when the patient is extremely dangerous to himself, hospitalization is unavoidable.) Larry will be discharged as soon as possible. A tragic mistake is to admit a child and keep him too long.

Larry wasn't aware that he was ill. "I didn't know but what everybody felt like I did," he said. "But man, when I started doin' drugs, I soon found that I could feel a whole lot better. And I'm not gonna make any promises to anybody when I get outta here."

Kids like Amy and Larry are self-medicators—they use drugs because they need them, just to get through each day. With these kids, improper diagnosis and treatment only results in an immediate return to drugs. They are so mixed up and angry that drugs are their only means of experiencing any kind of pain-free existence. There are thousands of kids like Amy and Larry.

They can't "just say no" to drugs. It is almost a physical impossibility. They need proper diagnosis and treatment which will alleviate their pain.

Larry Schmidt's father and mother met with me to discuss his illness. "I don't understand this bipolar problem you're talking about, Dr. Campbell," Mr. Schmidt said. "As far as I'm concerned, Larry is just a spoiled-rotten, smart-mouthed kid. His mother does everything for him. She's the one who spoils him to death. You know, if it wasn't for me, he never would have gone to work. I'm the one who insisted that he take that job he's got.

"But I guess it backfired on me, didn't it? I mean, maybe I should have taken away his allowance. Maybe then he wouldn't have had any money to buy his drugs with, and we wouldn't have been sitting here."

"I don't think you should blame yourself for that," I replied. "You see, Larry's illness is so painful for him at times that the drugs are the only way out. He would have found some way to get them."

"Dr. Campbell, I wish you wouldn't keep saying he is sick. I used to just slap him on the backside once in a while and that would straighten him out. Now, here we sit in this office talking about Larry being sick. I just don't know if I can agree with that."

"Hank," Mrs. Schmidt interrupted, "you said you would try to do what Dr. Campbell suggests. We almost lost Larry because nothing else has worked. Let's just try, at least."

Mr. Schmidt stood up. "I'm not going to make any promises, but I'll stick it out for a while. When are we going to bring him home from the hospital, Dr. Campbell? We're not made of money, and my insurance won't cover this kind of sickness."

"I'll tell you what, Mr. Schmidt. The more involved you and Mrs. Schmidt become in Larry's recovery program, the faster he will get well. I know that Larry's recovery is far more important to both of you than anything else at this moment. I do understand that money has to enter into Larry's treatment, so we are all going to do our best to help him recover quickly."

Borderline Personality Disorder

Those kids who suffer from borderline personality disorder display the maladaptive behavior of someone with a personality disorder, but they also have difficulty thinking clearly, logically, and rationally—symptoms of a thought disorder. They cannot be diagnosed clearly in either direction.

Kids suffering from borderline personality disorder have extremely poor self-esteem and self-identity. They often have a poor sense of values due to the fact that they can't think clearly. They have such a poor sense of identity that they usually have to attach themselves to somebody else in order to feel like a whole person. They often mimic other people in order to have an identity. They also develop an extreme dependence on someone. The borderline syndrome is a very complex syndrome, but we are beginning to learn more about it.

We are noticing a higher occurrence of borderline personality disorder in this generation than in past generations. The disorder usually results from extremes in negative child-rearing methods. A traumatized child almost always develops a borderline personality disorder. For example, whenever I see a sexually abused child, I usually see a borderline child. Of course, any kind of abuse or poor parenting can do it, but the most disturbed borderline personality disorder patients I have seen are kids who have received extremely poor parenting and kids who have been sexually abused.

Actually, any one kind of abuse will cause a child to develop borderline syndrome. Physical abuse, including inconsistent discipline, will cause this disorder. And these kids are prime targets for drug and alcohol abuse. When I first started practicing psychiatry, we seldom saw a borderline child. Now, this disorder probably ranks as the most common problem we are dealing with.

Drugs and the Borderline Child

Again, we see the necessity of understanding and evaluating the whole child in order to gain an understanding of his drug problem. It is imperative that a child's neurological condition be understood so that proper medication can be administered if necessary, or so that counseling can be given which will help the child to understand his problem. He needs help in developing a good self-esteem and a healthy self-identity so that he will not feel the need for illicit drugs.

A borderline child can actually be harmed if illicit drugs are taken away from him and he is not given appropriate treatment for his disorder. If a teenager's thought disturbance is severe enough, an immediate removal of drugs without proper treatment can cause his thought processes to become even more confused. Any kind of distraction can cause him to become illogical and irrational. In extreme cases, borderline personality disorder kids come to the point of having hallucinations like a schizophrenic person.

Stress affects these kids easily and causes erratic behavior. And since stress is never constant, their behavior is never constant. When the average person experiences stress, he still maintains an awareness of where he is and what he is doing. Not so these borderline personality disorder kids. The more stressful the situation, the more confused their thoughts become. Sometimes they appear to act normally, and then they suddenly become irrational. Their behavior constantly varies. You can readily imagine how miserable it would be to have a mind that is constantly changing.

These kids usually do pretty well in the classroom because it is structured. But when they get to the playground, they can become very confused and display inappropriate, even bizarre, behavior. An extreme, but very real example of such behavior would be for a borderline child to strike another child on the head with a rock or some hard object. The child with a borderline personality disorder might also throw another child off the top of a slide without even realizing what he is doing because he is in a confused state of mind, possibly even psychotic. (To be psychotic is to be totally out of touch with reality.)

Teachers see this all the time and rarely understand that they are dealing with a borderline personality disorder child. When the child sits in the principal's office, he appears normal. The reason for this sudden change of behavior is that when the child is put in a rather isolated room, the noise level is low, and he is not confused with a lot of stimulation. (The principal's office or counselor's room is usually isolated and quiet.) He is able to pull himself together as he sits and waits for the principal or the person in charge of discipline.

Finally, when the principal comes in and addresses the problem, the child appears to be perfectly all right. The child apologizes for his behavior because he truly does not understand why he acted the way he did. The principal sees a child who seems to be genuinely sorry for his conduct, so the issue is dropped and the child heads back to the playground.

Stimulation of any kind can cause the thoughts of a borderline kid to become disjointed and confused. This confusion causes painful feelings which can be worse than depression. The child can be utterly tormented. Drugs are a relief from this type of pain.

These kids usually experiment with drugs at a very early age. If they do not become addicted, they at least become dependent on drugs after their initial experimentation because drugs help them to keep their thoughts and emotions in order.

Kids with borderline personality disorder become adults with borderline personality disorder. When borderline adults try to define their feelings, they find it difficult to do so. They use words such as *foreboding, feelings of pending evil,* and *a sense of extreme blackness everywhere.* They say that at times they just can't get away from the pain of these feelings. They feel at times as if they are "covered with a black blanket."

Of course, the feelings may come and go, depending on the situation at any given moment and the degree of stress and stimulation the individual is experiencing. But when these feelings are extreme, the person will do anything to feel better. And drugs will block these feelings. We can see why people with borderline personality disorder may use drugs at an early age.

Joyce is an example of a borderline kid who started using drugs at an early age. She is now a twenty-four-year-old mother of two small children who has used drugs and alcohol since she was fourteen years old. She is a small, sad woman, and she is an alcoholic. She spent a bizarre childhood with two alcoholic parents.

"Dr. Campbell, I never knew from one minute to the next whether my parents were going to knock the stuffing out of me or hug me and maybe even read me a story. Even though they were alcoholics, they always managed to hold good-paying jobs, and we had pretty much what we wanted.

"My dad, though, he was a strange one. Sometimes he would scoop me up in his arms and laugh and tell me all about his day, and I would tell him all about what happened at school that day. Then, maybe only thirty minutes later, he would throw his shoe at me and knock me to the floor with his foot because I forgot to bring in the evening paper.

"My mother was just as crazy. I remember one time she made me a dress for my senior high dance. It was a beautiful thing. Anyway, she wanted me to try it on just as I was leaving the house for school, and I didn't have the time. I told her I would do it just as soon as I got home from school.

"That night after school, I found my dress on my bed, torn to shreds. I nearly died. Somehow, though, I tuned them out. I guess I just grew numb to their actions."

But Joyce didn't tune them out as well as she thought she did. She was unable to withstand such bizarre inconsistency. Her homelife was damaging to the point of creating a person with a borderline personality disorder in Joyce. She is a sick young woman, and her illness will be difficult to treat because she has relied on drugs and alcohol for so many years.

Treatment Must Involve the Family

Borderline syndrome, like depression, learning disabilities, and any of the problems I've been discussing in this book, is a family problem. If the family unites in seeking a cure, the prognosis is usually bright.

If the family does not work together, however, the child will have an extremely difficult time overcoming his disorder. Kathy is an example of a borderline person whose parents are not consistent in their involvement with her treatment. Kathy is eighteen and a tormented young woman. She has previously sought treatment for her drug addiction, but to no avail. She is now bulemic, has attempted suicide twice, and is still addicted to drugs.

I have placed Kathy in the hospital because of her bulemia and suicidal urges. Bulemia is an illness which exhibits the symptoms of extreme overeating and then forced vomiting. Bulemia, like drug addiction, is a symptom of a deeper psychological problem. So Kathy has three major problems: she has a borderline personality disorder, she is bulemic, and she is addicted to drugs. Every one of these problems is a symptom of a psychological problem.

When I first saw Kathy, she was in the hospital, and both her parents were with her. They seemed to be caring and quite interested in her welfare, but when I tried to set up a time schedule for family counseling, they began to have a number of excuses that would keep them from the sessions.

"Don't worry about them, Dr. Campbell," Kathy said. "They always do that when I get in trouble. They always pretend in front of the doctor how interested and loving they are, but they don't really mean it. They don't care what happens to me."

"Let's not worry about that right now, Kathy. Maybe you and I can talk for a while. Where would you like to start?"

As Kathy's story unfolded, the reasons for her illness became obvious. From what she said and from what the records showed, her parents offered little emotional support. They didn't seem particularly interested in her. But, as Kathy said, they were supportive of her brother. And the fact that they didn't attend any of the scheduled family counseling sessions due to their son's ball games further supported Kathy's statements. "It's probably because I'm fat and ugly, and he's skinny and good at sports that they don't like me. I don't know. I do know I tried for a long time to please them, but it never does any good.

"Mother is always on me about something. Clean up your room. Lose some weight. Fix your hair. Get a job. That's all I ever heard from her when I was at home."

"You say, 'when you were at home.' Where do you live now, Kathy?"

"Mother threw me out last year, so I am living with a friend. First I moved in with my aunt and uncle, but that didn't work out. I guess you already know about that, Dr. Campbell."

Yes, I knew about that. Kathy's uncle had sexually molested her repeatedly when she was staying there. She finally tried to tell her mother about it, but her mother couldn't or wouldn't believe her.

"I guess you know that my brother molested my little cousin when he was fourteen and she was five," Kathy continued. "My mother and dad sure hurried right off to a counselor then. They just knew that nothing was wrong with their wonderful son, and they were going to prove it in a hurry, I guess. At least they went to three or four sessions with him. That's a lot more than they have gone to with me."

As I counsel with Kathy, I do not wonder that she has borderline personality disorder and is bulemic. And I can understand that she tries to escape her tormented existence by using drugs. The irony of all this is that her parents are seemingly bright people, both of whom hold responsible jobs, yet their parenting skills are practically nonexistent.

Kathy will have to be hospitalized for some time yet. She has a long way to go before she gains some insight into her problem. She has very poor self-esteem. She is still very bulemic. She bribes her friends into sneaking candy to her so that she can binge and then induce vomiting.

Treatment Must Consider the Whole Child

Kathy's case is an extreme example of self-medicating to ease the pain of her illness. Incorrectly diagnosed in the past, Kathy is in real danger now. Her past treatment has consisted of short-term hospitalization, a few counseling sessions, and a warning to stay away from drugs. Kathy honestly tries to do what her counselors say, but she cannot. She is too ill. Her case again points out the absolute necessity of the whole child approach to treating a drug problem. Kathy's drug problem must be treated by helping her with *all* of her problems.

To diagnose Kathy's problem as simply a lack of communication with her parents combined with a little peer pressure and warn her about continual drug use is totally absurd. And that is exactly what has been going on. No wonder she is in her present state of mental and physical health.

We have completed a full evaluation of Kathy. We have contacted her high school where she is a senior, and her teachers are cooperating by arranging to get her homework to her. She is strongly involved in group therapy sessions. And, above all, we are going to continue to try to get her parents involved. If they do not play an active part in her treatment, Kathy will find it extremely difficult, though not impossible, to get well.

I hope this chapter has helped you understand yet another reason for a child to become involved in drugs. Again, early intervention and treatment is best for these children who have mental/neurological disorders. The older these kids are when diagnosed, the greater the probabilities that they have suffered serious emotional scars. But I assure you, they are treatable. Please don't despair.

This chapter concludes the chapters of discussion on specific reasons kids use drugs. It is difficult to pinpoint any one reason, as you can see. Anger and depression are two of the major reasons for drug abuse. And then add the pain of a learning disability or a bipolar affective disorder, and we can well understand why a child turns to drugs.

Treating Your Child's Drug Habit

In this chapter I will discuss specifically what to do if your child is involved with drugs. It's always bad news when you discover that your child has a drug habit. The good news is that something can be done about it. Your family will be healthier and happier when all of you pull together to fight the problem.

Let's start with another true-false exercise. At this point you should be able to answer most of these questions correctly.

True   False

1. All kids know exactly why they use drugs. They're just too stubborn to talk about it.
2. There is usually one single reason why a child becomes involved in drugs.

3. Most parents, by themselves, can cure their child's addiction to drugs.
4. Teens have a difficult time identifying the feelings within themselves.
5. Family involvement is an important issue in the treatment of drug problems.

So far we have discussed the source of drugs and the world our kids live in. We have also talked about anger, depression, learning disabilities, and other reasons why kids become involved with drugs. Now I am going to try to help you arrive at some solutions to your child's drug habit. Often, just seeing how other people solve their problems can be a big help, so I will tell you how Larry Schmidt, Peggy Williams, and Johnny Alton are getting along. You will remember them as the three kids whose stories started this book.

Larry Schmidt didn't know why he used drugs. He only knew they made him feel good. Larry's bipolar affective disorder was the prime reason for his drug addiction. A thorough evaluation of Larry gave us immediate insight into his illness, and now we are working with Larry and his family to help him stabilize his life.

Larry is still very defiant. He is filled with anger. For example, during Larry's last visit he became argumentative. "I'll tell you what, Dr. Campbell, I don't see why drinking a beer now and then can hurt anybody," he began. "I have a lot of friends who drink a beer or two, and it don't hurt them a bit."

Drinking beer would be harmful to Larry for any number of reasons. The fact that he is on a specific medication for his illness is one major reason. Mixing his medication and alcohol could be physically harmful as well as harmful to the progress of his treatment. One beer would surely set him on the road to drug use and eventual abuse, and we would all be back to step one. The fortunate aspect of Larry's situation is that his parents are beginning to become involved. His father, especially, had great difficulty understanding that Larry was dependent on drugs, but now he is beginning to understand.

During their last visit when Larry brought up the beer issue, Mr. Schmidt became angry. "I sure wish you'd get your head on straight pretty soon, Larry," he said. "Sometimes you worry your mother and me half crazy, especially your mother."

"Yeah, but what am I supposed to do? Just sit around like some wimp all the time and say 'Yes, ma'am' and 'No, ma'am.' "

"Is that what your mother and dad ask you to do?" I asked.

"No, you know they don't, Dr. Campbell. I just get mad when people tell me stuff to do all the time. I can make a few decisions on my own once in awhile."

"Do you think deciding to drink beer is wise, Larry?"

"I don't know."

I could see that Larry was becoming agitated. I changed the subject. I knew that recently he had begun guitar lessons. "How's the music coming along? Still enjoying it?"

"Yeah. Might start a group. My instructor thinks two or three of us are good enough to do a few things for school assemblies and stuff like that."

Larry's problems are not solved, but at least we are working on them. We have included his family physician and his teachers in his treatment, and I feel that we are making progress. A much earlier diagnosis would have made a world of difference in Larry's life. Drugs would probably not have become such a strong part of his life.

Now Peggy Williams, on the other hand, was brought to us in the early stages of her drug problem, and her mother has been quite supportive of her. A thorough evaluation and subsequent counseling sessions have given all of us the much needed information which offers insight into her troubles.

"You know, Dr. Campbell," Mrs. Williams said during one of our sessions, "if I had only known from the start that Peggy was a 25 percenter, life could have been so different for her. She always seemed to be such a well-behaved girl. I never realized how much she was keeping inside. One good result, aside from Peggy being so much better, is that her younger sister is benefiting from all of this. But I still feel so guilty when I think of the pain Peggy suffered due to my ignorance."

That is one of the most common statements I hear. I assured Mrs. Williams that she shouldn't continue to feel guilty. "Look at how far you've come. Peggy is doing well, and the two of you have had this chance to really get to know each other for the first time in your lives. You only did what you knew how to do at the time. Allowing guilt to take over now will only cause you to take a backward step. And Peggy certainly doesn't need that. She is making great progress."

Mrs. Williams' face brightened. "I guess you're right, Dr. Campbell. At least I know my family a whole lot better now, and we are happier than we've ever been. Oh, we argue and do a lot of stuff we've always done, but I know which traps to stay out of now. And I know that when trouble arises, I can call you."

I am pleased with the progress this family has made. They've worked hard to get where they are today. But Johnny Alton concerns me. Even though his father came into my office telling me that he had attended two A.A. meetings, I don't feel that he was fully aware of his or Johnny's problem. A.A. is a tremendously helpful organization, but Mr. Alton needs some counseling to go along with the meetings.

I seek spiritual guidance every day of my life, and this family is in my prayers. I am pleased to note that Mrs. Alton is becoming more aware of her past position in her family, and she appears to be asserting herself more. She is becoming a strong support for Johnny.

I just wish that Johnny's life could be a little easier for him, but the world of the learning disabled child can be tough. Johnny has learned a lot about himself, though, and at least he has the support of his mother. Life is beginning to turn around for him.

The main point I want to bring out in discussing these three kids is that none of them understood why they were taking drugs. Our evaluations not only taught us about these kids, but they also helped these kids to become aware of themselves. Teens have an extremely difficult time identifying their inner feelings. None of these kids realized that their association with drugs usually stemmed from unconscious motivations. As a matter of fact, few people realize that most decisions in life are based on unconscious motivations.

We make almost all of our decisions primarily based on the way we feel. Kids feel down or bored, and they may use drugs to feel better. They don't go through a thoughtful, rational thought process to make that decision. Drugs make them feel good, so they do drugs. They do not truly understand why.

People rarely try to figure out a correct decision; they simply justify their feelings and convince themselves that they are right. This is called rationalization. Both kids and adults rationalize.

Rationalization is the reason why drug treatment can be so difficult. Anyone who doesn't get acquainted with the whole background of the child and his drug problem is really just rationalizing, determined to see a child's drug habit only the way he wants to see it. The child, the teen, the parents, and the teachers all may think they have the answer, and they are determined to prove themselves right.

The Damage of the Single Diagnosis Theory

Anyone who thinks he has the corner on understanding drug abuse is "barking up the wrong tree." No single person knows everything there is to know about drugs. The wise person will have an open mind and try to see the entire picture of this complex problem. The problem is not just a physical addiction, and it's not just doing something because "the devil made me do it." It's an extremely complex issue.

Parents often feel helpless. They don't know whom to consult. All they know is that their child is using drugs, and they want this habit stopped. The desire to cure their child overnight is the reason so many parents fall prey to "the single diagnosis theory."

To further emphasize the confusion and pain that can be caused by the single diagnosis treatment, to say nothing of the damage to the drug user, let me tell you about Polly Lanning.

Polly's 18-year-old daughter, Lana, had spent two years in and out of various treatment centers and under the care of many different counselors before she came to me.

Polly came alone for the first visit to our center. She had quite a story to tell.

"I'm here alone, Dr. Campbell, because I want to tell you what the last two years have been like and to ask you if there is anything left to be done for my daughter. I love her, and I want her health and well-being to improve, but I don't know where to turn anymore.

"I am going to start at the beginning, and you can jump in at any time. Maybe between the two of us, we can help her. I hope so. Let's see—first of all, I have been married three times. My first marriage ended because I was very young when I married and I didn't know how to cope with a stern, demanding husband. That marriage wasn't a total loss though because my first daughter, Marie, was born then. My second marriage ended because my husband, Lana's father, was an alcoholic. She was six years old when we divorced. I did not remarry until six years later when I met, and fell in love with my present husband, Hal. He is a wonderful person and very good to both my girls. He has three grown children, none of whom live with us.

"Lana was twelve when Hal and I married. We moved from the town she grew up in to our present home at that time. She seemed to handle the move quite easily. She always made friends readily, so a new neighborhood and a new school were no problem to her. She entered the seventh grade the year we married, and the first two years were relatively uneventful. During her freshman year in high school, she was voted class president, and things still seemed fine.

"It was during the second semester of her sophomore year that I noticed a subtle difference. She had been elected president again that year, but she began to complain of the job, saying that she was going to give it up. I noticed that her group of friends had changed, but she gave such good reasons for the change that I really didn't question it at the time.

"Then she announced one evening after school that she had

given up the class presidency, making the excuse that she got no cooperation from anyone. She just quit. I had never known her to lie before, so I believed her. But one change occurred that caused me to question Lana.

"You see, Dr. Campbell, I always had both girls place a list of friends' names and phone numbers on our refrigerator. After Lana's friends changed, her list became small and finally nonexistent. When I questioned her about this, she said that her friends' families were odd, or didn't have phones, or just any old excuse.

"Finally I realized that something was wrong. It was late in the second semester of her sophomore year that she cried out for help. She had been coming home late from school. Twice she didn't come home at all, and we had to send the police out to look for her. The second time she did this, she had been out all night, and when we found her, she asked us to help her. She told us that she was using drugs and that she wanted help. So we immediately placed her in a treatment center, and that began our two years of trying to help Lana.

"She was placed in the maximum security section of the center because she had attempted suicide. But she talked somebody in charge into letting her have a gym pass, and then she and another girl just walked out the door. Hal and I went immediately to the hospital to find out what we should do."

"How did you find her? Did you place her back in the hospital?" I interrupted.

"Oh, yes. While we were at the hospital, the father of the other girl called and asked to talk with us. He said he had Lana with him and that she was fine, but that she didn't want to go back to the hospital. He said, 'I'll tell you where she is if you'll promise that you won't take her back there.' So I made that promise, picked her up, and drove her back to the hospital."

"How did she react to that?"

"She was violent. She cursed and spat at me, accusing me of lying to her and betraying her. But Dr. Campbell, I didn't know what else to do. According to what we had learned from the hospital, she told them that she had tried every drug possible and, of course, she had attempted suicide. I knew that I had a mighty sick girl on my hands. We weren't getting along at all at home, so I had to bring her back.

"At the hospital, I inquired if any kind of diagnosis had been made, and they told us that Lana had a bipolar affective disorder. I had never heard of this problem, and when I asked what it was, I was told that it is a condition which causes mood swings. I certainly could agree with that because that is what we had been seeing in her at home."

"How drastic were these mood swings?" I asked.

"Well, Dr. Campbell, she would go from an overtalkative, giggling girl to an extremely depressed person who threatened suicide. So anyway, I asked if anything could be done for this and was told that she should take Lithium."

"Where was her biological father during this time? Did he agree with your actions?"

"He did happen to come into town the day we found her, but he didn't show any particular interest. His main concern was when we thought she would be getting home from the hospital. I guess maybe he was worried about whether or not his insurance would hold out. I will give him credit for giving her financial support, but he certainly hasn't given her emotional support."

"How long did she stay in the hospital?"

"We admitted her during the middle of March and brought her home on June 1st. Her psychiatrist had prescribed Lithium, and I thought we were going to get along fine. Things weren't too bad. We counseled weekly. Her psychiatrist felt that her bipolar disorder was not as important to deal with as the fact that she and I didn't get along. He dwelt mainly on trying to teach us to communicate. I worked hard. I felt so guilty. I really believed that her entire problem was the result of poor parenting on my part. Hal was extremely supportive of me and he too attended the counseling sessions.

"But we just didn't seem to be getting anywhere. Then one day a friend asked me how often Lana was being monitored. I didn't even know what she was talking about. Then she told me that her brother was bipolar and that he was monitored regularly because he was taking Lithium. By this time, Lana had been taking Lithium for almost six months, or so I thought, and no one had said one word about monitoring her.

"I called her psychiatrist, and he said he would do some tests. It was then that we discovered that she hadn't been taking the Lithium at all. I was so angry with her. Everything fell apart again. I quit taking her to this psychiatrist, and she asked if she could go back to the psychologist she had seen on a daily basis in the hospital. I took her. What a disastrous mistake that was!"

"What do you mean by that?"

"For example, after she had been seeing him for about a month or less, I would ask her to help with simple chores about the house, such as folding a load of laundry. She would react with 'No, I don't have to because I don't want to. My psychologist says that whatever I think and feel is right and that I should go with my feelings.'

"So I called him and asked how this approach was going to help her. He reminded me that I had been tearing down her confidence and that he was working very hard to rebuild it. I knew I wasn't tearing her down, and I didn't see any improvement in her mood swings, so I quit taking her to him. After that, our old habit of arguing began to return. And now Lana had added to her verbal expressions of anger, some attempts to physically strike me. Also, her mood swings were getting worse. Just when I was looking for someplace else to take her, she tried suicide again.

"She had been pouting around the house all day, and I really don't remember why. But, at any rate, as I was preparing for bed that evening, she came into our room and announced that she had taken an overdose of some kind of pills and that we should just leave her on her own bed to die. Needless to say, we rushed her to the emergency room of the hospital. Our family doctor tended to her physical needs and suggested we come talk to you.

"I am ready to throw in the towel. I don't know what to do. If I am totally at fault, I will do anything to change what I can and try to live with the rest. I do want her to be healthy. She won't take her Lithium. She says it makes her feel too bland. I think she really likes the highs she experiences due to her illness. I don't know. It's all one awful mess. I've tried extra for almost two years to do what her psychiatrist and psychologist said. They both seemed to think that her main problem is me. Oh, and I took her to one other psychologist who told me that she is an abused child."

"Is she?" I asked.

"Definitely not. At least she's not a physically abused child. And if she's mentally or emotionally abused, I certainly didn't do it consciously. You can't imagine the guilt I have lived with. I felt so guilty about being divorced twice that I tried extra hard to be a good mother. I tried to compensate for the pain the divorces caused both girls. Maybe all those psychiatrists and psychologists are right. Maybe everything is all my fault. What can Hal and I do?"

"I'll tell you what, Mrs. Lanning. We're going to do everything we can to get to the bottom of this. We are going to do a complete evaluation of Lana. We will be needing her school records and her previous hospital and mental health records. In the meantime, you shouldn't blame yourself. You and your husband can relax in the knowledge that we are going to try to help. Lana, indeed your entire family, has suffered from these years of trial and error."

The Lannings' situation is a perfect example of how the single diagnosis theory can be more harmful than helpful. In this case Mrs. Lanning was given most of the blame for the problem when she was not the primary cause of the problem. It is unfortunate that Lana's bipolar affective disorder was not considered as a major cause of her addiction because it *is* the primary cause.

After doing a thorough evaluation on Lana, we found that her bipolar affective disorder has, indeed, been one of the main reasons she started using drugs. This illness, along with her natural adolescent passive-aggressive actions and the mishandling of the entire situation has created some real problems for Lana and her family.

We are just beginning to work with this family, but I do feel hopeful. Lana's mother and older sister and her stepfather and his children are all working together to help her. They are all attending some family counseling sessions whenever they can.

This is a strong family unit and if Lana will cooperate, we'll be able to help her. Lana's case certainly points out the need for early detection and intervention.

I am frustrated when I hear prominent sports figures saying, "Hey, it's peer pressure that makes kids do drugs." This message may cause parents to force their children to quit being with their friends, which may only compound the issue. Kids need friends.

Some professionals will promote the single diagnosis theory by saying, "You're going to have to let go of him a little more and give him some freedom. Communicate and trust." This, more often than not, results in a child having too much freedom, a perfect way to stay involved with drugs.

Peer pressure does play a role in a child's experimentation with drugs. Some parents do hold their children too tightly. Some parents don't communicate with their children. But none of these factors by themselves are the initial cause of drug use. It is almost always a combination of these factors and more that causes a child to eventually become addicted to drugs.

Parental Drug Use

According to an article in a magazine for teenage girls, psychologists in Santa Monica, California are finding that kids whose parents use drugs are prone to using drugs: "Probably the biggest factor I've noticed common to kids using drugs is the kids with parents who are active users of drugs or alcohol" (Wendy White and Karle Dickerson, "Teen Drug Dealers Uncovering the Real Story," *Teen*, Feb. 1988, p. 37).

This fact is evident in the story of Todd whose mother abused drugs and alcohol for fourteen years. Todd is an intelligent young man. He is now a senior in college. He is planning to be married after graduation, and his fiancée is the person who convinced him to seek counseling for his own drug problem.

"It hasn't been easy, Dr. Campbell," Todd began. "I was about seven when Mom had her gallbladder operation. I guess it was after that operation that she started abusing drugs. You see, her doctors allowed her an unlimited amount of painkillers. She kept her supply of drugs going by complaints of back problems and later nervous depression and frustration. All the while, my father, my brother, and I watched her go deeper and deeper, but we denied the problem and accepted her excuses for using drugs.

"I remember very little of the early years of her disease. I do remember knowing that there was some kind of a problem, but I did not understand what it was. The only memories I have of my middle childhood years are terrible ones. I remember lying awake night after night listening to the screaming and arguing between my parents. At that time, I didn't realize that the reason for the arguments was Mom's use of drugs. For some reason, I blamed myself for these arguments. I would lie awake and cry because I couldn't figure out what to do.

"By the time I reached my teens, I knew that Mom had a problem with drugs. But along with the rest of the family, I continued to deny the problem.

"By now, I had been keeping the house up for two or three years. I felt that I was being cheated out of my childhood. I did everything I was told to do because it was the only way that I knew I could keep peace in the household.

"In high school I started to learn about drug abuse. I began to push my father and older brother to put Mom in the hospital for treatment. At the same time, I was using my growing freedom that comes with age to avoid going home until I had to. When I would go home, I would stay in my room and watch television or read a book. I only felt good when I was not home or Mom was on the road, working at one of her many short-lived jobs.

"I had no hope for Mom. As far as I was concerned, I felt that we should just put her away. Anyway, she said that same thing many times. But my father never gave up. He and my maternal grandmother kept pushing until they finally got Mom to go to a halfway house in our town. It is run by the Alcoholics Anonymous organization. The people there saved my mother and my family. She has been clean for about a year now, and she and Dad are putting their lives back together.

"And Dr. Campbell, that's why I'm here talking to you. I want to put my life back together too. I am beginning to be able to love my mother again and, as you know, I am getting married this summer. As a matter of fact, if it hadn't been for the beautiful woman I am marrying, I might have ended up like Mom. My future wife understands me and my problem."

Todd's family did what most families of drug abusers do; they denied that the problem existed. And along with this denial, they (especially Todd's father) lectured and nagged at the abuser in an attempt to get her to stop. They acknowledged the problem and attempted to deny it at the same time. The whole family wanted to maintain the illusion, "A nice family like ours does not have degenerate alcoholics and drug abusers."

Todd said that he could see his father falling into the hands of the disease, totally defenseless and confused. Nobody could do anything. This is another common occurrence in these sad situations. The spouse finds himself covering debts and trying to hold the family together. He constantly tidies up after the alcoholic.

"Things were awful, Dr. Campbell. My father just became a workaholic. He spent every day and every night at his store. In looking back, I guess it was a way to escape my mother's problems. Oh, he tried to spend time with me now and then, but work was his escape."

Children in substance-abusing families grow up feeling alone, for many reasons. They are unwitting victims of a disease they cannot control. It shapes their personality and controls their behavior on into adulthood. They have little chance of escaping the disease without help from others. Todd became a substance abuser.

We are finding that children of substance abusers take on one or a combination of the following four roles: the responsible child, the adjuster, the placating child, and the defiant child.

As Todd mentioned earlier, his first role was that of the

responsible child. He kept the house in order. He also tried the third role for a while. He tried to keep peace between his parents regardless of the personal cost. This and the second role, the role of the adjuster, are quite similar. The adjuster is flexible. He tries to go along with whatever is happening, just shrugging when plans are changed at the last minute because of the substance-abusing family member.

Todd eventually took on the fourth role; he became defiant and began to use and abuse illicit drugs himself. When he met the young woman he will soon marry, he began to see things differently. He is now attending counseling sessions regularly, along with his fiancée and his family.

Todd is a strong young man, and he will probably make it. But many kids of drug-abusing parents suffer some enduring effects. They have a tendency to drop out of school in larger numbers than other children; they are at a greater risk of developing emotional and physical problems; they have more drug and alcohol related problems; and they often have difficulty trusting their feelings, which creates a problem in achieving lasting relationships with peers and others.

Drug Use and the Lack of Spirituality Theory

If a child grows up knowing that God truly loves and cares about him, and if he sees God as a positive authority figure instead of a negative one, then spirituality is a very strong force in helping him resist drugs. Sadly, many teens today have a negative view of God because of harsh parental disciplinary measures and an overemphasis on religion. I certainly agree that spirituality is important in rounding out a child's life, but lack of spirituality cannot be the single, initial cause of drug abuse. Preaching at kids with a drug habit definitely will not help the situation.

Recently, I became acquainted with an organization which claims that lack of spirituality is the main cause of drug abuse. This organization does not even recognize unconscious motivation as a factor. They claim an 80 or 90 percent cure rate of all their patients. They simply say that anyone who finishes their program is cured. But any kid can finish a treatment program and still not be cured. Unless all areas of his life, including the spiritual area, have been examined and treated, he is likely to go right back to his old habits. How sad that this organization condemns any other kind of treatment.

Only a Thorough Evaluation Results in Effective Treatment
If you have a child with a drug problem, I encourage you to seek out a person who is involved with a treatment center which works with the whole child. A complete evaluation of every area of the child's life is imperative. You should be wary of any one person or organization that condemns all types of treatments except their own. Again I say, I do not have all the answers, but I *do* know that rarely does one single reason induce a child to use drugs. Physical, neurological, psychological, and unconscious factors are all involved in drug addiction, and the child and his parents need to become aware of these in each individual child.

Parents are never in a position to prevent drug use or stop current drug use unless they have a broad picture of the entire situation. It is the only way to really help your child. I don't mean that you have to know absolutely everything about your child. That's next to impossible. But the more you know about your child, the more you will be able to help him with the problem areas in his life.

We must remember that the teen does not know for sure why she is using drugs. She has a difficult time understanding her inner feelings. All these terrible feelings within her make her hurt and unhappy, so she will use drugs to feel better.

Peggy Williams is a perfect example of using drugs to ease her pain and unhappiness. She wanted to express anger, but didn't get to. She did not consciously realize that she needed to express anger; she only knew that she was unhappy and drugs helped.

I can't stress enough how very critical it is to understand the total picture. How in the world can these kids be treated if we don't fully understand their personalities, their lifestyles, their worries, and the kinds of stress they are experiencing?

When we evaluate a patient, we gather information about academic history, birth history, family history, emotional history, relationships with peers and parents, and anything else that we can possibly find out.

Next, a psychological evaluation is in order to find if there is any unconscious motivational factor. The evaluation is also needed to determine whether or not the patient is depressed and the extent of the depression. Sometimes depression will become obvious in conversation, but the *amount* of depression cannot be measured just by talking to the patient. It is also difficult, but not impossible, to measure just how much unconscious, submerged anger a child has and how much of this is coming out in passive-aggressive behavior.

Now, when all of this data is compiled, we have the whole picture, and we can sit down and talk with the child and listen to the child. Teens, especially, can be taught so much about themselves if someone will take the time to talk and listen.

Teens today experience a tremendous amount of pressure. That is why now, more than ever before, teens need to know about themselves. They need to know what type of personality they have, why they think the way they do, and how they feel and why they feel that way. They need to understand unconscious motivations, the internal drives that make them do things that they really don't realize they're doing. Most important, teens need to become aware of both their assets and their liabilities.

When we do a thorough evaluation, we are not only finding out what is going wrong in the child's life, but we are educating him about himself. And this is so very critical.

If your child is experiencing a drug problem and is receiving treatment without a thorough evaluation and a diagnosis, he is not receiving the proper attention. It is always very distressing to me to see a professional sitting alone in an office trying to treat teens who are on drugs, especially those with neurological problems.

For example, let's look at the problems of the hyperactive

child. I, or anyone else, simply cannot treat the hyperactive child without input from other professionals. He needs individual counseling. He needs counseling with his parents and siblings. Often, the hyperactive child needs a specific medication, and this medication needs to be monitored. This is also true in the case of the bipolar affective child and sometimes the child with borderline personality disorder. A single diagnosis of the hyperactive child is useless because he will go back into a home where no one understands his problem.

If your child has a drug problem, seek a treatment center which includes psychiatrists, psychologists, social workers, special education teachers, and other professionals. I cannot stress enough the absolute importance of this type of treatment. It is impossible to diagnose the drug problem, treat only that physical addiction, and help the child. His problem always goes far deeper.

I hope I have fully explained the needs of the drug-addicted teen. I hope you will be able to look objectively at your drug-addicted teen and your family dynamics and arrive at a treatment program which will benefit the entire family.

I worry a lot about whether or not my boyfriend is going to ask me to smoke marijuana. I know he does and I don't want to, but I don't want him to quit me.

Janice, age 16, high school sophomore, drug-free

Keeping Your Child Drug-free

The title of this chapter expresses the ideal of every parent: to have your child abstain from drugs in a drug-mad society. Abstention is the only sure method of preventing addiction.

Before we get into this last chapter, please read the following statements. As you reflect on these facts and the contents of this chapter, you will better be able to plan a family program for keeping your child drug free.

1. Alcohol and drug abuse occur more often in parent controlled settings than anywhere else.

2. Parents rarely learn from negative parenting skills they received as children and carry these negative aspects over into the lives of their children.

3. Parents should never *force* their children to attend

church; it is one sure way to create feelings of anger and frustration.

4. As kids get older, parents have a tendency to give them less verbal and physical affection.

5. Verbal and physical affection are just as important to an adolescent as they are to a smaller child.

6. Early intervention into any childhood problem is extremely important.

7. Unconditional love and consideration of the fact that your child is an emotional, psychological, spiritual, and physical being are the most essential ingredients in raising physically and mentally healthy children.

8. Parents should not depend wholly on their child's school to solve his drug problem.

9. In 1986 a study of 8,000 fifth- through ninth-graders revealed that 1 out of every 4 fifth- and sixth-graders had used alcohol in the previous twelve months and 1 out of every 10 reported being drunk once or more during the previous twelve months.

A note from the *Reader's Digest* is in order at this point before I start this final chapter by telling you about Brad.

The hardest part of raising children is teaching them to ride bicycles. A father can run beside the bicycle or stand yelling directions while the child falls. A shaky child on a bicycle for the first time needs both support and freedom. The realization that this is what the child will always need can hit hard (O. Sloan Wilson, "Points to Ponder," *Reader's Digest*, February 1986, p. 181.)

When Brad was three years old, he indulged in a major temper tantrum because his mother would not buy him a toy. "Oh, get it for him," his father intervened. "After all, he's the baby of our four. We probably won't have any more children, so let's enjoy this one."

When Brad was eight years old, he was verbally abusive to his teacher and refused to do his schoolwork. His parents went to talk with his teacher. "We're going to do all we can to see that this doesn't happen again," his mother assured the teacher.

"I think we're all taking this thing much too seriously," his father interrupted. "After all, he's only eight years old. When I was eight, I hated to sit in a classroom all day long. I think we can ignore the whole thing. He's a smart kid. And I want to enjoy this one. There's no need to get him all upset over nothing."

When Brad was fourteen, the principal of his school called his parents. "I need to talk with both of you," he requested. "Brad is having some trouble here at school." The next day, Brad's parents went to school.

"I guess you know by now," the principal began, "that Brad was seen putting his hands down the front of his girlfriend's blouse, and he has been caught smoking marijuana here at school."

"Yes," his mother answered, "and we are quite upset about it. We are going to seek counseling for Brad."

"Now wait a minute," his father addressed the principal. "Brad is just all male. Have you seen that little gal he dates? Come on, weren't you ever fourteen and in love? And as far as that marijuana goes, Brad has told me all about that. He was just holding it for a friend. Why, look at his grades. He's a great kid and really quite intelligent. I've enjoyed this one more than the other three put together, and I'm going to keep on enjoying him."

Brad is twenty-one years old now. He is totally addicted to drugs and alcohol. He has wrecked three of his father's vehicles. He has never held a job. He attends college for no more than a semester at a time and then drops out because, to quote Brad, "I need to rest awhile. Those profs load it on too heavy." Then he moves back home and uses his college money for drugs.

Brad is a patient of mine. His parents faithfully attend all our family counseling sessions. His mother is willing to go along with a treatment program we have designed for him, but his father won't hear of it. Brad's father is still making excuses for him. Even his siblings (two older sisters and one older brother, all in their early thirties) come to some sessions, but we aren't getting very far because his father can't seem to let go.

One evening, during a family session, Katie, the sister closest to Brad in age, said to her father, "Dad, you have to turn loose of this boy. You are supporting his drug habit by allowing him to use that money for drugs instead of school. When are you going to wake up and throw him out on his ear? He's going to have to learn to sink or swim."

"Now, Katie, I can't just throw him out. He can quit those drugs whenever he wants, don't you think so, Doc? There's a good chance he'll soon just outgrow this whole thing."

"But he's twenty-one, almost twenty-two now, Dad. Don't you think he has had enough time to grow up? He depends on you and Mom for everything. He's going to spend every dime you have, and then what are you going to do?"

"Now, Katie. That's no concern of yours. You have your own family to care for. We'll take care of Brad. He's still just a kid. Sure, he's had his problems, but we love having him right here at home."

"It's no good, Dad. You've bailed him out of every mess he's ever gotten himself into. You've finished everything he's ever started. He's never even had the privilege of failing."

During this entire conversation Brad sat across the room soaking it all in with no apparent reaction. I suppose he had heard it all before. But when he left the room for a few minutes, his father turned to Katie and said, "Listen, daughter, Brad is a sensitive boy, and I wish you wouldn't talk like that in front of him. Your mother said he has been talking a lot about suicide lately. Don't you see? We can't throw him out? How would you like to have his suicide on your hands? I, for one, could not stand it—I simply could not live with it."

Sadly, Brad did try to commit suicide just a few days ago. He took an overdose of drugs and washed them down with alcohol.

Brad's story fits with that of many teens who end up in a treatment center for drug abuse. They are there because they simply lack the tools for living. Throughout their lives, people have taken care of them. When these kids are teens, they experience the same loneliness, fear, pain, pressure, setbacks, and disappointments that any other kids experience, but they are never taught to cope with these emotions and frustrations. Someone always intervenes and copes for them. Brad's sister was very wise when she suggested that Brad should be allowed to fail. After all, how can he ever experience the joy of winning if he never suffers the pain of losing?

Homelife Shapes Adolescents Behavior

What young adolescents become and how they behave are strongly tied to life at home. Research finds that family closeness, parental nurturance, parental affection, and authoritative discipline are closely associated with the lack of antisocial behaviors and drug abuse. On the other hand, authoritarian control, coercive punishment, and less nurturance have been linked with a series of less desirable behaviors.

Brad received no type of discipline, and his family was obviously not a close one. His father overindulged his every whim. His mother and his siblings were constantly in direct disagreement with his father concerning how Brad was being raised.

On more than one occasion, Brad's father bought him alcohol so that he could have his beer parties at home. He rationalized that it would be much safer than having him out on the road, yet he gave no consideration to all the kids who would be driving to the party.

Studies show that parents must play a more active teaching, modeling, and monitoring role in the lives of their children. Even though alcohol and marijuana are used in school settings, they are used more often in settings more appropriately under the control of parents, such as, parties, weekends, and summer vacation (*Source*, Vol. II, No. 3, Search Institute, August 1986).

I too am a parent so I know from firsthand experience the

problems and pitfalls of parenting. I know that raising children in today's world is so difficult that it is entirely possible to be an above average parent and still have trouble with your child.

Unfortunately, children do not arrive with a computer print-out entitled, "An Eighteen-Year Maintenance Plan for This Model." Parents are left on their own to do the best they can. I know I have talked a lot throughout this book about the role parental nurturance plays in the mental health of a child, but a good fact to remember is that behavior patterns begin at birth. Consequently, while the initial actions of the child may not be the fault of the parent, the reaction of the parent is of the utmost importance.

Some children are truly difficult to raise. About 15 percent of all children are born with difficult personality traits. Parents of these kids must keep on their toes and exercise special care to prevent emotional or behavioral problems from arising later in the life of the child. This is where parental reaction must be carefully monitored. Some characteristics become stable features as the child grows. (I mentioned 25 percenters and 75 percenters in chapter 3.)

Many children are fairly easy to raise. They seem to eat and sleep regularly and are generally easy to console when they become upset. Other children are going to react intensely to the smallest change. Research has not come up with any answers as to why these personality features appear. Heredity is the most popular theory. These traits seem to appear with about the same regularity and frequency in all families and all societies.

The key to child rearing is to consider all of these different traits normal. A fussy child is just as normal as a complacent child. It is the parental response to these various personalities that determines whether the child develops positively or negatively.

Trying to change a child's personality can and does cause problems that pervade his life. He may grow into an angry, depressed, disobedient adolescent. Parents must manifest love for their children regardless of their various personalities. Of course we want to alter inappropriate behavior, but we must respect each child's personality regardless of what it is. When a child is constantly criticized and told that he is a problem child, he will become one.

Now, let me give you a few guidelines to use during these sometimes wonderful, sometimes terrible years of child rearing. These guidelines will help you help your child avoid drugs.

Know Yourself

First of all, before you can be totally effective as a parent, you should know yourself. Let's go back to Johnny Alton. If Mr. Alton had been aware of his own learning disabilities, maybe life could have been completely different for that entire family.

Most learning disabled adults do not fully understand their problem. They may think they lack intelligence. They have difficulty, the same as children do, in understanding expressions of love and care due to this handicap. This lack of understanding creates a feeling of low self-esteem which is a negative concept to carry into parenting. As one young mother said to me, "Dr. Campbell, how can I love my baby when I don't even love myself?"

Far too many parents also do not understand that they still have some passive-aggressive traits. They do not realize that they are still filled with unresolved anger from their adolescent or earlier childhood years. As a consequence, their anger is vented on their spouses and their children. It would be beneficial for you, at this point, to determine whether you are a 25 percenter or a 75 percenter. This knowledge can help you in dealing with yourself, and it can help you determine which personality trait your child has. Once you have this information, a multitude of problems can be prevented.

Parents also carry negative parenting skills learned from their own upbringing into the lives of their children. For example, we learned while counseling with Larry Schmidt's family that Mr. Schmidt had been physically abused as a child. And he has used severe physical punishment as a means of reprimanding his own children. Until he can come to a full understanding of the negative parenting skills of his own parents, another generation of children will be harmed. Parental self-awareness is a most invaluable tool to have.

Love Your Child Unconditionally

Regardless of personality, hair color, or size, your kid must be loved. Love is the primary need in your child's life.

Let me tell you about Lori. She is, by today's standards of physical beauty, a very plain girl. She is of medium height, but overweight. She has a bad case of acne. Her mother is a very attractive woman and, according to Lori, was an extremely popular and beautiful teen. She even won her school's "most beautiful girl" award. She was a cheerleader and the junior prom queen. Lori feels inadequate because she constantly compares herself to her mother as a teen. Furthermore, Lori is kept constantly aware of the mother's past accomplishments and popularity.

"My mom is forever telling me all about how many dates she had to turn down and how she never had any trouble keeping her hair looking nice. I think she just says that because my hair is just like Daddy's—fine and oily."

Lori is a quiet, 25 percenter. This personality trait, added to her mother's constant nagging, has resulted in serious depression for Lori. She has turned to drugs to ease her pain.

"Oh, I don't think my mom loves me," she said to me one day. "How could she? She is beautiful and I'm ugly. She was popular in school, and I only have one real friend. Besides that, I've never been out on a date."

Lori's mother is a selfish woman. She has not bothered to become acquainted with her daughter. She has offered her little love and support which Lori so desperately needs. No adolescent, regardless of her assets, can develop in a healthy manner without unconditional love from parents. All adolescents feel insecure, and Lori is getting a double dose of insecurity. She already feels it naturally because she is an adolescent, and then her mother constantly belittles her. It is no wonder she is depressed.

Model Your Beliefs

A third, and immensely important rule to follow in your home is to allow your Christian beliefs to be evident in your daily life. It is your model of Christianity more than your verbalization of Christianity that your child will follow.

When your children are small, they will attend church and Sunday School with you and enjoy it. But when those adolescent years roll around, your child may suddenly rebel against going to church. It is not his rebellion against spiritual matters that can cause the trouble; it is your reaction to his rebellion. Don't become alarmed. Just continue your regular attendance habits, keeping your Christianity obvious in your life, and soon your adolescent will follow. But patience is the key word here. Don't use threats and promises to force your adolescent to go to church with you. You will only push him away when he becomes an adult. Just wait him out. He is only rebelling because he is an adolescent, and adolescents must always rebel against some authority figure. In time, he will see your sincerity in your beliefs and will follow you back to church. He will also follow your Christian lifestyle when he becomes an adult. This is one area where your reaction to his action is very crucial. As long as he feels unconditional love, he will experience self-worth. An emotionally healthy child who knows her parents love her will want to follow in her parents' footsteps.

Communicate with Your Child

Kids are bombarded with so many negative, anger-causing situations that they need a parental sounding board. They need to talk with their parents in order to alleviate their fears and anger. Encourage your child to talk with you, but don't try to force him to talk. Nothing closes the doors of parent-child communication any faster than a parent who insists and demands that his child talk.

Be patient. All kids hate silence and will eventually begin a conversation. I have found that a long trip in a car, for example, will eventually bring out your child's desire to talk. He may not start discussing his problems initially, but if you wait long enough, you will soon hear his concerns.

Teens may appear to have no need for their parents, but appearances can be deceiving. They do need you and long for you to be involved in their lives. As I mentioned earlier, kids in a strong, supportive family situation are less likely to engage in harmful behavior such as drug and alcohol use.

Consider All Your Child's Needs

I always encourage the parents who counsel with me to consider that their children's needs are many. They are not just psychological and emotional beings. They have physical needs and spiritual needs also. A child whose physical needs are well-tended, but whose psychological, emotional, and spiritual needs are practically ignored, will become a troubled child.

Pam is a pretty, blue-eyed, fourteen-year-old who overdosed on drugs. Her father is a corporate executive, and her mother operates a successful, privately owned business. Pam appears to have everything.

Her parents are strict in an authoritarian way. She is told everything she must and must not do. She is not allowed to talk back or argue in any way with either of her parents. She is not allowed to question the actions of her parents or her teachers because, she is told, they are always right. She is forbidden to miss church. Any display of emotion is a sign of weakness; therefore, she must not expect praise.

As you can see, Pam appears to have everything, and yet she has nothing. Her psychological, emotional, and spiritual needs are being ignored. Only her physical needs are being met. But Pam cannot function with this kind of parenting. And her parents sincerely believe that their strict, authoritarian attitudes will prepare her to face life. They are not considering that she lacks any self-esteem. They are giving no thought to her own unique spiritual life. Obviously, they are not developing the whole child. Pam will have a difficult time recovering from her drug habit with parental attitudes such as these.

Pam's predicament reminds me of a story in which a boy came home from school one day and said to his father, "I love you." In this family "I love you" was such a foreign statement that the father did not know how to respond, so he asked his son, "What is it you want?"

The boy only laughed and said, "Oh, nothing, Dad, just an experiment for one of my classes at school. My teacher told us all to come home and tell our parents that we love them and then report the reactions. You reacted like almost every other father; you didn't know what to say."

A study of fifth- through ninth-graders indicates that as they entered their teen years, they began to receive less verbal and physical affection from their parents (*Young Adolescents and Their Families*, Search Institute Project Report, 1984, p. 31). Ironically, these parental expressions of love are absent at a time when they are most needed for the healthy development of the child. It is imperative that parents love their children if a well-rounded, drug-free adult is to emerge.

A little note from *Reader's Digest* ("To Arms!" August 1987, p. 166) seems appropriate at this point.

> Hugs are not only nice; they're needed. Hugs relieve pain and depression, make the healthy healthier, the happy happier and the most secure among us even more so.
>
> Hugging feels good, overcomes fear, eases tension, provides stretching exercise if you're short, and stooping exercise if you're tall. Hugging does not upset the environment, saves heat and requires no special equipment. It makes happy days happier and impossible days possible.

What a great statement! And who do you know who has more impossible days and needs a daily hug any more than an adolescent?

Early Intervention Is Crucial
A final and very important aspect in effective child rearing is early intervention when a problem is suspected. We have

learned that every kid is unique, and no parent can do a perfect job. But we can, at least, intervene early when we see a problem arising. Early intervention can save years of pain and suffering.

Fifteen years ago, I might not have been as concerned about early intervention as I am now. I would have told parents to make sure that certain specific needs were being met, and I would have felt comfortable that the child would soon be fine.

Today, young children are experiencing so many problems that I would like to see each one of them evaluated as early as first grade. Just imagine the problems we could identify and nip in the bud. With early detection of a problem, no matter how insignificant, a plan of action could be implemented immediately and years of frustration avoided. It is much better to err on being overcautious than to wait until the problem develops into a situation that is difficult to handle. For example, it is much easier to help a twelve- or thirteen-year-old who is messing with drugs than a fourteen- or fifteen-year-old who is involved. Sixteen- to eighteen-year-old kids are even more difficult to help.

We as parents and counselors have our hands full. It is amazing how complex a problem can become during the time span of only one year. We need to be constantly aware of our children. The best of all situations for any child is unconditional love and a stable, loving home. If all parents could give this to their children on a daily basis, about 80 percent of childhood problems could be avoided. Then an awareness of the signs of learning disabilities, depression, and passive-aggressive behavior could eliminate another 10 to 20 percent of childhood problems. Wouldn't that be wonderful?

Helping Your Child Refuse Drugs

Drug and alcohol use is a major national problem. We must all face the fact that at some point almost every child will come into contact with drugs and have to make a decision about whether or not to try them. We need to help our children prepare for these encounters.

Someone tossed the following list on my desk the other day. Some of the statements are comical while others are quite serious, but any one of them could help your child refuse an offer of drugs or alcohol.

1. "My parents wait up for me, and they smell my breath every night when I get home."
2. "If I get caught, my mother will take away my hair dryer!"
3. "I'm allergic to it."
4. "If you drink or do drugs, you get zits!"
5. "I don't want to lower my chances of having healthy children when I grow up."
6. "Friends who do drugs together don't have a very deep friendship—drugs are all they have in common."
7. "I don't want to support the grower-to-user chain—there are some pretty bad people involved in drug dealing."
8. "I'll become an alcoholic because that runs in my family."
9. "It's against my religion."
10. "I tried it once, and I got sick."

Search Institute's January 1986 publication of *Source* lists several important components in preventing adolescent chemical abuse which echo the guidelines for effective parenting which I've already given you.

● *Parental expectations.* In one of their studies, Search Institute found that chemical users responded with less concern than nonusers did to a question about "how upset would your parents be if you came home from a party, and they found out you had been drinking?"

● *Social networks.* The degree to which adolescents are involved in adult-supervised programs and activities is another factor which inhibits drug and alcohol use.

● *Social competency.* A number of social skills, all of which can be promoted by family, school, church, or other organizations, can serve as important factors in prevention. These include friendship-making skills, communication skills, decision-making skills, and the ability to say no when peer pressure does enter the picture. (I might add to this finding that all of these skills can be developed in the child who comes from a loving and stable home.)

● *Personal values.* Adolescents who refrain from alcohol and drug use, in comparison to other youth, are more committed to educational achievement, more involved in people-helping activities, more confident that the future holds promise, more affirming of religion, and more able to resist immediate gratification of needs.

It is apparent that these components of a drug-free life can be achieved by consistent and loving parenting. Combine a stable homelife with community interest in assuming some responsibility for a drug-free environment, and your child can lead a drug-free life. It is no easy task, but it is so important.

I am always sad when I read statistics such as the ones contained in number nine at the beginning of this chapter. It is alarming to read that 1 out of every 4 fifth- and sixth-graders in our nation has not only tried alcohol, but has been drunk. I have hope, however, that we can bring these numbers down.

Remember Johnny Alton? Because of his mother's concern, love, and determination, and his own desire to overcome his addiction, Johnny is doing well. We are working with his school and teachers and receiving full cooperation. Johnny's reading ability has not changed, but he is learning how to cope.

And remember Larry Schmidt? Larry's father was having a problem dealing with the whole situation. Well, Mr. Schmidt kept coming to our counseling sessions and has finally developed an understanding of his son's illness. I am so very pleased to report that this family is making major strides toward a better life.

Peggy Williams and her family are doing well too. At first, Mrs. Williams felt that she was the total reason for her daughter's involvement with drugs. As we talked, however, she soon understood the whole picture, and she and her daughters have benefited tremendously from their sincere involvement in Peggy's treatment.

As you have noted by now, I strongly urge all parents to first arrive at and treat the causes of drug involvement and then treat the drug problem. Treating the whole child and helping him to understand why he became involved with drugs is the key to restoring his health. The rest of the family members also gain an insight into their own personalities. This treatment almost always helps the other family members to remain drug-free. With everyone working together, whole families are helped.

Although I am gravely concerned about the prevalence of drugs in our society, I am still hopeful. I have faith in you as loving, caring, parents, and I know that you want a drug-free life for your child and will do all that is in your power to help him. It is for parents such as you that I have written this book.

| APPENDIX 1 |

Information about Cocaine

The Great Deceiver: What Parents Must Know About Cocaine

Until recently, cocaine was perceived as a relatively safe drug. Although health officials did not believe it was completely harmless, they thought the social problems associated with cocaine use were remote to most American families. Most parents thought cocaine might be a problem for celebrities and sports figures, but not for their children. *We now know that cocaine is an addictive, intoxicating substance with potentially fatal health effects.*

With the recent deaths of a number of star athletes and other notables, however, the perception of cocaine has changed. Research now shows that even small, so-called "recreational" doses of cocaine appears to trigger dangerous and potentially fatal heart disturbances in seemingly healthy users. In other words, cocaine can kill you!

An Overview

Cocaine is a chemical extracted from the leaf of the coca plant, a South American shrub. The shrub stands three to six feet tall and yields about four ounces of leaves during the largest of the year's four harvests. Its waxy, elliptical shaped leaves are about 1 percent cocaine by weight.

A colorless or white, odorless crystalline powder, cocaine appeared in the Untied States in the mid-19th century. Physicians began investigating its medical applications for what many regarded as a wonder drug, a safe cure for a variety of physical and psychological maladies.

Eventually, physicians and scientists built a solid enough case against the indiscriminate use of cocaine to have it labeled a narcotic. Today it is classified as a Schedule II drug under the Controlled Substance Act—it has legitimate medical uses but a high potential for abuse. The legal manufacture, distribution, and use of cocaine are tightly controlled and monitored.

Its use in medicine today is limited to a highly diluted local anesthetic by ear, nose, and throat specialists and proctologists.

Gaining Popularity

Each year, growing numbers of teenagers begin using cocaine. While the overall use of illicit drugs by teenagers continues a gradual decline that began in 1980, their use of cocaine continues to increase.

In a 1975 University of Michigan study, 9 percent of the high school seniors surveyed said they had used cocaine at some time in their lives.* Ten years later, that number was up to 17 percent. In 1986, it was about the same, at 16.9 percent of 15,000 students surveyed. Those who indicated in the survey that they

---

*NOTE: The survey of high school seniors does not measure the drug use patterns of high-school-senior-aged students who have dropped out of school. Thus, these figures may be lower than for the entire 18/19-year-old population which would include those who have dropped out of school as well as those still in school.

had used cocaine in the past 12 months rose from 7 percent in 1975 to 13 percent in 1986.

However, the number of high school students admitting to being daily users of cocaine doubled between 1985 and 1986 surveys (0.2 percent—0.4 percent). The survey also found cocaine use up among all groups of teenagers: males and females, college-bound or not, urban and rural, and in every region of the country.

An analysis of data obtained through interviews with 100 callers to the 800-COCAINE hot line found that the "typical" teenage user was a white (83%), male (65%) high school junior or senior (average 16.2 years). Over a third came from families with annual incomes over $25,000; many were from middle and upper class homes. Almost 9 out of 10 snorted it, 10 percent smoked it as freebase, and 2 percent injected. Most used other drugs to counteract the unpleasant effects of chronic or high-dose uses—marijuana (92%), alcohol (85%), sedative-hypnotics (64%), and heroin (4%).

It had been assumed by most experts that cocaine's high price would prevent teenagers from becoming involved with the drug. However, in recent years authorities have seen a sharp drop in its price. In some heavily populated urban areas, the price has declined by a third in the past two years alone, making it available to many who could not afford it before. In New York City, a gram of cocaine, enough for 10 doses, sells for about $80 on the street. Most teenagers know where to get cocaine, and a group might pool their money to get high. Some dealers are selling it in quantities smaller than "eighths" (of a gram), making cocaine affordable for any teenager with the interest to try it and $10.

Forms of Abuse
Cocaine Powder. Most casual users of cocaine inhale it through the nose, or "snort" it. A small quantity of the powder is placed on a mirror or other flat surface, chopped with a razor blade to remove flakes and lumps, and formed into "lines" or "rails" one to two inches long and ⅛-inch wide. The cocaine is inhaled

through a straw or rolled-up currency. Lines average 25 milligrams of cocaine, 60 percent of which is absorbed through the mucous membranes of the nasal passages into the body. Inhaled, the drug's effects peak in 15 to 20 minutes and disappear in 60 to 90 minutes.

Coca Paste. Coca paste is a precursor compound (a substance from which another substance is formed). It is frequently smoked in combination with tobacco and/or marijuana, producing an intense effect similar to cocaine or amphetamine injections.

Freebase. One of the most dangerous forms of absorption of cocaine, second only to intravenous injection (see "Intravenous Solutions"), is smoking the freebase. Freebase is a form of cocaine which is made by chemically converting the "street" cocaine hydrochloride, by using volatile chemicals, into a substance that is suitable for smoking, and that is more pure than the cocaine powder sold on the streets. It is typically smoked with a water pipe. Smoking freebase produces a shorter and more intense "high" than most other ways of using the drug because smoking is the most direct and rapid way to get the drug to the brain. Because larger amounts are getting to the brain more quickly, an intense rush is produced. Smoking freebase can cause severe psychological symptoms to develop rapidly. These symptoms often require hospitalization.

"Chasing the dragon" refers to another method of smoking cocaine that includes using heroin.

Rock Cocaine. In the 1970s, a new form of cocaine emerged called "rock." It is a small chunk of cocaine hydrochloride which was initially believed by its users to be free of any adulterants.

Rock cocaine is typically white and is about the size of a pencil eraser. Rock cocaine is used for intranasal snorting.

Crack. Another smokeable form of cocaine, crack, was first reported as an East Coast phenomenon, but is now found throughout the country. It is spreading both to more rural and to poorer areas. Two properties make crack uniquely popular among teenagers.

First, like rock, it is cheap and easy to make. Crack is formed by mixing cocaine hydrochloride with baking soda and water. This mixture creates a paste which, when it hardens, is broken into small pieces resembling soap chips or professionally pressed into small pellets. These pellets are sold for $10 to $15 a piece and are extremely potent. Crack reportedly has the same potency of freebased cocaine without the danger of fire and explosion that might be caused by the volatile chemicals used in the freebasing process.

Second, crack is highly addictive. This form of cocaine is five to ten times more potent than cocaine powder. It reaches the brain in less than 10 seconds. The resulting euphoric high lasts about 15 to 20 minutes, and is followed by a crushing depression. The depression causes the crack user to crave another hit to the drug within a few minutes after taking the first one.

Intravenous Solutions. Some users inject a cocaine solution under the skin, into a muscle or a vein. Intravenous use is often preferred as it is the only route that yields 100 percent absorption of the drug. The result is an intense high that crests in three to five minutes and wanes over 30 to 40 minutes.

If the user shares needles with another user, there is a risk of acquiring hepatitis and/or the human immunodeficiency virus (HIV) which causes AIDS—Acquired Immunodeficiency Syndrome. Over half of the AIDS patients reported since 1981 have died. The HIV also causes a syndrome called AIDS-related complex, or ARC, in which the victims' immune systems are impaired to a lesser extent than with AIDS. It is estimated that there are 10 times as many ARC cases as AIDS cases in the United States, and about one-quarter of these cases will develop into AIDS. There is no cure for AIDS or ARC.

Other Forms. Cocaine can also be eaten or rubbed onto the gums for the taste and numbing sensation.

Its Effects

Cocaine can be absorbed through any mucous membrane, and is carried by the blood to the heart, lungs, and rest of the body. Inhaled, it reaches the brain and neurons of the sympathetic nervous system in three minutes; injected, in 15 seconds; smoked, in seven seconds. The chemical is metabolized rapidly by the blood and liver. Its actions on the sympathetic nervous system mimic the body's fight-or-flight response to fear or challenge.

Cocaine is a vasoconstrictor; that is, it narrows the blood vessels. The heart rate, blood pressure, and respiration are quickened and the body's metabolism is stepped-up. The user's appetite is deadened and he cannot sleep while intoxicated with the drug, or "high." Cocaine stimulates at least two areas of the brain—the cerebral cortex (which governs high mental activity such as memory and reasoning), and the hypothalamus (which is responsible for appetite, body temperature, sleep, and certain emotions).

Cocaine's effects are similar to those of amphetamines. In fact, subjects in research studies cannot distinguish between the effects of the two at lower doses, except that amphetamines' actions are longer lasting.

The extreme euphoria associated with cocaine use resembles that produced by direct electrical stimulation of the reward centers of the brain. But what goes up must come down. With cocaine, as with other stimulants, the higher the high, the lower the low.

The euphoria and excitement of the initial "rush" taper off—gradually when used intranasally, quickly when injected or smoked, and the user slides into a physiological and psychological depression. This state is characterized by a "let down" feeling, dullness, tenseness, and edginess. A listing of symptoms is included later in this text.

Cocaine sold on the streets of America declined in purity from 1978 until 1982. However, purity is on the rise—jumping from 29 percent to 73 percent from 1982 to 1984 as shown by one California study. The price has dropped to pre-1977 levels despite increased purity. The fatal dosage for an average-sized adult used to be considered 1.2 grams; however, some individuals have died recently from 1/60th of that amount, or 20 milligrams.

Symptoms of Abuse

There are telltale signs of **cocaine use:**
- frequent sniffing or nose rubbing
- dramatic weight loss over a short time
- coughing up a black mucous
- unexplained chest pains
- high blood pressure
- vascular disorders
- losing interest in friends, sports, or hobbies
- declining grades in school
- symptoms of depression
- restlessness, irritability, anxiety, or sleeplessness
- hallucinations of touch, sight, taste, or smell

Death from overdose, accidents while impaired, and suicide during depression are possible.

Withdrawal Symptoms

- depression
- social withdrawal
- drug craving
- tremor
- muscle pain
- eating disturbances
- changes in the electrical patterns of the brain ("brain waves") as measured by a medical testing machine called an electroencephalograph (EEG)

Withdrawal symptoms can motivate the cocaine addict to resume using cocaine.

Prevention

Research is starting to show that the best method of preventing drug use is to teach people, especially children, how to recognize and reverse the pressures within society to use drugs—peer pressure reversal or *how to say no!* This is a common-sense approach long advocated by the NFP. Teaching someone about the health effects of various drugs and building self-esteem are important components to a peer pressure reversal-based program, but by themselves they are not as effective as programs that involve parents or peers. Providing information about the clinical effects of a drug simply provides information. It may scare some for a while, and others will focus on one "desirable" effect while ignoring more serious hazardous effects—just as an acquaintance who uses will do. Self-esteem-building is useful, but does not provide the knowledge or role playing practice of how to say no that a sound peer pressure reversal-based instruction program will do. Resources are available through the NFP which can help adults and youth learn the techniques for successful peer pressure reversal. See the NFP's catalog of publications for a complete, up-to-date listing.

Treatment for Cocaine Users

Treatment for any form of cocaine use should focus on immediately stopping all drug and alcohol use. Oftentimes, treatment will require hospitalization, especially for the crack user because of the more intense drug cravings and the more serious psychiatric and medical problems resulting from using the drug. After initial detoxification, inpatient treatment consists of counseling, support groups, and family therapy. Long-term aftercare is essential to continued sobriety, or to remain "clean" of cocaine. Cocaine users who are treated as outpatients will require an extremely structured and intensive program with daily counseling sessions, immediate family involvement, and urine testing at least three times per week. Substitute drugs or gradual detoxification cannot be used.

For more information about treating a child on cocaine, consult your local pediatrician or your family doctor. You may want to seek a referral to someone specializing in the treatment of addictions.

The following are the national offices for non-professional, support groups for individuals who are using cocaine and want to stop, and for their family members.

For the cocaine user:
Cocaine Anonymous World Service Office
P.O. Box 1367
Culver City, CA 90232

For family members:
Cocanon World Service Office
Box 3969
Hollywood, CA 90028

Sources of Information:
Gabriel G. Nahas, M.D., Ph.D. (President of the International Medical Council on Drug Abuse, and Professor of Anesthesiology, College of Physicians and Surgeons of Columbia University).

National Strategy for Prevention of Drug Abuse and Drug Trafficking— 1984 (Drug Abuse Policy Office, The White House).

University of Michigan, Institute of Social Research, Survey of High School Seniors data (National Institute on Drug Abuse).

Eric Voth, M.D. (Director, Chemical Dependency Treatment Center, St. Francis Hospital, Topeka, KS).

Drug Abuse and Drug Abuse Research (The second triennial report to Congress from the Secretary, Department of Health and Human Resources), DHHS Publication No. (ADM) 87-1486.

| APPENDIX 2 |

Information about Marijuana

What Parents Must Learn About Marijuana

Many teenagers often refer to marijuana as a natural, harmless weed. Yes, marijuana is natural, and it is a weed, but research shows that it is far from being harmless. In fact, it is the most chemically complex of all the illicit drugs.

Marijuana (also called pot, grass, reefer, herb, or weed) comes from the *Cannabis sativa* plant. This plant is divided into three types: the fiber type, which is used to make rope and paper; the intermediate type, which produces neither good fiber nor, in its unrefined state, potent marijuana; and the drug type, which is most often used by teenagers today.

Typically, the marijuana used in cigarettes (joints) is made from the drug type—a mixture of leaves, small stems, and the flowering tops of the Cannabis plant. Other parts of the plant are also intoxicating. Hashish (hash) is a green, dark brown, or black sticky juice that is extracted from the plant and pressed into cakes or slabs. It is also smoked to produce a high. Hash oil, a tarlike substance usually smoked in small amounts on tobacco or marijuana cigarettes or in small glass pipes, is another extract of the plant. It may be even more potent than marijuana.

How Does Marijuana Affect the Body?

In the 1970s, marijuana was thought to be harmless. This prompted pro-marijuana groups to call for decriminalization and even legalization of marijuana. It's "harmlessness" was based on inconclusive studies, plus the fact that the number of smokers was far less than today's and the strength of marijuana was much lower. Today, there are many researchers, psychiatrists, psychologists, doctors, drug counselors, educators, and former users who testify to its danger.

Evidence now shows that marijuana contains 421 chemicals, including delta-9-tetrahydrocannabinol (THC), the one which produces most of the "high." When marijuana is smoked, the burning causes its 421 chemicals to turn into 2,000. When the body tries to metabolize them, hundreds more are produced. Recent studies have shown that after one use of the drug, 10 to 30 percent of the THC consumed still remains in the body up to 30 days. Continued use results in further accumulation in the body's fatty tissue. This accumulation, especially in high concentrations, can destroy body cells.

Marijuana smokers usually experience:
- reddening of the eyes,
- dryness in the mouth and throat,
- decreased body temperature,
- increased heart rate,
- a sudden appetite.

In addition, the THC in marijuana affects hormones that control sexual development, fertility, and sexual functioning in both sexes. In males, marijuana lowers testosterone, the principal male sex hormone; decreases sperm count; causes abnormalities in the sperm; and, in a few cases, enlarges the breasts. In females, marijuana disrupts the menstrual cycle, in some cases causing failure to ovulate. A large number of women smoking marijuana have offspring who show altered visual responses, marked tremors, and a high-pitched cry like that of newborns of heroin and methadone addicts.

Recent studies by the National Institute on Drug Abuse (NIDA) show that the drug impairs short-term memory, alters sense of time, and reduces the ability to perform tasks requiring concentration, swift reactions, and coordination. High doses may cause image distortions and hallucinations.

While marijuana may not directly cause mental problems like many other drugs, it appears to bring to the surface emotional problems and can trigger even more severe disorders. People suffering from depression and other emotional disturbances who use marijuana often experience a worsening of the problem. Over 5,000 people seek professional help every month for problems related to marijuana use.

Perhaps the most disturbing effect of marijuana use is its possible interference with growing up. As research shows, the effects of marijuana can interfere with learning by impairing thinking, reading comprehension, and verbal and arithmetic skills. Researchers also believe that the drug may interfere with the development of adequate social skills and may encourage a kind of psychological escapism. Teenagers need to learn how to make decisions, to handle success, to cope with failure, and to form their own values and beliefs. By providing an escape from "growing pains," marijuana prevents teens from maturing and developing independence and responsibility.

What Can You Do?
Drug use by one family member affects every other family member to some degree. As a result, many parents adopt their own methods of coping with the problem. However, many of these coping behaviors are insufficient and do not restore family cohesiveness. To achieve the best results, parents must acknowledge that a drug problem exists, provide examples of the pain and suffering it has caused within the family, and unite in an unwavering effort to help the drug user overcome the problem.

Although some teenagers can extricate themselves from drug dependence, it is unlikely that such a resolution will occur without some professional help. Therefore, if you suspect that your teenager is using marijuana, seek guidance from a counselor experienced in drug rehabilitation or a minister, psychologist, or physician knowledgeable about drug dependency.

In addition, call the parents of your teenager's friends and discuss how each of you can help raise drug-free children. This parent group phenomenon is being called the most successful drug prevention method available. Discussion should evolve around setting limits for appropriate behavior for your teenagers and defining consequences for violations of those limits.

Remember, the drug problem can only be solved by taking away the customers. This begins in the home. Drug prevention in the 1980s is not easy work, but it can be done.

Did you know:

- of the teenagers who smoke marijuana, one in three becomes a daily smoker?
- sometime between the ages of twelve and fourteen, nearly every American teen is faced with the choice of whether or not to smoke marijuana?
- nearly 60 percent of all high school seniors surveyed have smoked marijuana at least once; one in 18 smokes marijuana daily?
- the younger the marijuana smoker, the heavier and more persistent the use will be?
- more than one in every five students has admitted having problems as a result of smoking marijuana?
- of the 421 chemicals in marijuana, 103 of them are terpines which are very irritating to the lungs?
- newborn babies exposed to THC, through their mother's use of marijuana, had some subtle developmental abnormality?
- today's marijuana can be about 14 to 20 percent stronger than marijuana used in the 1960s?
- surveys conducted by NIDA show that 60 to 80 percent of marijuana smokers questioned indicated they sometimes drive

while high?

(Taken from *What Parents Must Learn about Marijuana*. Reprinted by permission from the National Federation of Parents for Drug-Free Youth. For additional information write to: National Federation of Parents for Drug-Free Youth, 8730 Georgia Avenue, Suite 200, Silver Spring, MD 20910.)

| APPENDIX 3 |

Information about other Current Popular Drugs

Alcohol—A colorless, volatile, pungent liquid which is the intoxicating element in whiskey, wine, beer, and other fermented or distilled liquor. Increased use creates increased tolerance.

Amphetamines (uppers, speed, bennies, dexies, pep pills, diet pills)—Synthetic stimulants with effects similar to those induced by cocaine. Some popular brand names include Benzedrine, Dexedrine, and Methedrine. These are controlled substances which are legal only if prescribed by a medical doctor.

Heroin (smack, horse, skag) or other narcotics (methadone, morphine, codeine, or Dilaudid)—Narcotics which are particularly addictive. These narcotics or synthetics narcotic drugs are potent painkillers. The substance common to all narcotic drugs is opium.

Inhalants (glue, aerosols, amyl nitrite, butyl nitrite)—When inhaled, these substances create effects that range from mild intoxication to visual hallucinations. These substances are said to provide many children's first exposure to consciousness-changing drugs. They are relatively easy to obtain "over the counter."

LSD—A psychedelic drug which comes in a variety of forms including tablets, capsules, gelatin chips, and blotter (paper).

PCP or Angel Dust—A synthetic compound which is often called an anesthetic, but unlike anesthetics, is not a depressant. The mental effects are variable but often include a feeling of disconnection from the body and from external reality, apathy, disorganization of thinking, a drunk-like state, and distortions of time and space perception. Overdoses can cause convulsions and coma. When smoked, PCP produces effects that come on within a few minutes, peak within five to thirty minutes, and last for four to six hours. The effects of oral doses may last longer, and some people say they do not feel normal for up to twenty-four hours after a single oral dose.

Quaaludes (ludes, sopers, methaqualone) or **barbiturates** (downers, goofballs, yellows, reds, blues, rainbows)—Central nervous system depressants, primarily prescribed for insomnia and sedation. Quaalude is a brand name drug composed of methaqualone, a substance which produces similar effects to barbiturates.

Tranquilizers—Function like barbiturates to calm people down. They are prescribed mainly for anxiety disorders and muscle spasms. Librium and Valium are common brand names.

(*"Report on 1983 Minnesota Survey on Drug Use and Drug-Related Attitudes,"* Search Institute, Oct. 25, 1983, pp. 44–45. Used by permission.)